Grieve

Stories and Poems
about Grief and Loss

Volume 8

Grieve Volume 8
Hunter Writers Centre
PO Box 494 The Junction
Newcastle NSW 2300

Email: publishing@hunterwriterscentre.org
Website: www.grieveproject.org

Grieve: Stories and Poems about Grief and Loss

ISBN-9-780648-850403

Cover design by HWC Publishing
Typesetting by HWC Publishing
2020 Published by Hunter Writers Centre Inc.

How long till the nights
transform from shattering collision
to become the bruises
I know I can bear.

~

Under the Sun - Judy Johnson

Introduction

We will remember 2020 as the year of collective grief. For Australians, in particular, we began the year grieving—for our native forests and wildlife. The clean-up had just commenced and another wildfire arrived, this time sweeping the world. This anthology, the 8th volume of Grieve, contains personal experiences of the bushfires and the virus. These writers have unpacked the unfathomable for many of us. And other writers published here, against a background of a world perhaps forever changed, share with us their private losses: bedside vigils, job loss, loss of country, loss of child, post natal depression, cancer in remission, cancer in its final grip. These pieces were delivered with such profundity that we are left gasping and sometimes weeping. Weep away.

> *The world is indeed full of peril, and in it there are many dark places; but still there is much that is fair, and though in all lands love is now mingled with grief, it grows perhaps the greater.* — Lord of the Rings, J.R.R.Tolkein.

We hope this collection deepens your love for your neighbour, your workmate, friends and family.

We thank consulting judges, Peter Boyle and Heather Taylor Johnson, who selected the poems. We thank the judges from the grief and loss industries who, every year, read all the entries into Grieve and face the hard task of selection. Many of these judges face loss every day in their workplaces—as health workers, grief counsellors, palliative care specialists or funeral service staff. They have faced an extra challenging year in 2020 and we thank them for all their efforts with this project.

Congratulations to the writers awarded the 28 prizes donated by our sponsors without whom the Grieve project could not continue. A special thank you to Trudy Hanson OAM, CEO of the National Association of Loss and Grief. Generous of heart, a wise woman of many talents, Trudy retires this year after a lifetime of service to the people of Dubbo, the Central West and all of Australia through the Grieve Project.

Karen Crofts
Director
Hunter Writers Centre

Contents

Awards

The National Association of Loss and Grief (NALAG) Award
Invisible Ink - Sam X. Tan

The National Association of Loss and Grief (NALAG) Award
Pinwheels - Edwina Shaw

The Pettigrew Family Funerals Award
Word Search - Beth Clapton

The National Association of Loss and Grief (NALAG) Award
Eucalyptus citriodora - Gina Mercer

The Pettigrew Family Funerals Award
Lullaby - Eryn Purcell

All About Grief Award
Chantelle - Kim Langcake

Palliative Care NSW Award
The Last Swim - Allison Jeffries

Lake Macquarie Memorial Park Award
Under the Sun - Judy Johnson

Quest for Life Award
The Space In Between - Kaylia Payne

Simplicity Funerals Award
Verandah - Sam Morley

David Lloyd Funerals Award (Newcastle and Hunter Valley)
The Old-Fashioned Habit - Dani Glatz

Good Grief Award—for a work about grief or loss other than death
Kindness - Linda Harding

The Compassionate Friends Award
Key Change - Fiona Lynch

Newcastle Memorial Park Award
Always the Music - Jackie Tritt

White Lady Funerals Award
After - Janet Lee

The Calvary Mater Hospital Pastoral Care Award
Update on Lulu - Linda Godfrey

Interflora Award
In the long run - Marjorie Lewis-Jones

In Memory of Nathan Charles Richter
Small Steps - Hannah Trot

'Our World' Awards
Goodness - Chloe Warren
Fire Once Applied to Feathers - Jessica Valvasori

Newpsych Psychologists Award
How to Make Sage Butter - Chloe Brien

In Memory of Maree Richardson
Someone Put the Kettle On - Jean Kearney

The Canteen Award
Phone-calls and Waterfalls - Anthony Williamson

Maclean's Booksellers Award
Moments - Kelli Hawkins

The Blue Knot Foundation Award
7 White - 1976 - John O'Callaghan

Hunter New England Health, Mental Health Services Award
Your Call to Heal - Susan Tattersall

Hunter Writers Centre Award
Vessels - Scott-Patrick Mitchell

Mindframe Award
The Story of Us - Megan Brown

Invisible Ink

Sam X. Tan

'Sarah! Come, I wanna show you something!'

It's odd how memory works, Michael. We spent seventeen years in the same house, two decades scraping each other's knees and bickering over Dad's cookies. Still, when I think about you, it's always this one night that floats to the surface.

'SARAH!'

I remember walking in to our room, slightly resentful at having to pause *Crash Bandicoot*. The lights were out. You were hunching over the desk, tracing over the oak with a dense black pen. Only, when I looked, there was nothing there.

'Ta-da! Watch this!'

I remember you twisting your fingers, dousing the table in light. I blinked—and just like that, pirates and polygons were dancing, leaping, blooming to life under your ultraviolet sun.

'Isn't it cool, Sarah? Don't you think it's cool?'

But I was a Big Girl then, and so I withheld my surprise. I would end up dismissing you for the next ten years.

I remember how you used to show off your drawings, day after day, and each time I would devise a new excuse to ignore them. Eventually you started hiding and then you were locking yourself in your room after school, trusting only your sketchpad for company. Sometimes we would go for weeks without talking. But still I was too proud, too stubborn, to acknowledge you.

It really was cool, Michael. Why didn't I ever tell you?

I remember driving to hospital at ten in the evening. *Head-on collision at 65 kilometres. One passenger, aged seventeen. Both unrestrained.* By the time we reached your body, you were already gone.

That was twelve years ago. I live in Brisbane, now, and I'm a scientist by trade. I have a husband and two cats. But I still have memories of you, Michael.

I remember writing a uni paper on fluorescence, how certain molecules emit light when exposed to energy of specific wavelengths. For you, I thought—and there you were, reading over my shoulder. You didn't stay for the conclusion.

I remember coming home from lab, turning in to a cosy suburban road. You were standing by the bus stop, all grown up now, a charcoal beard silhouetting your jaw. I finished the drive with my palms shaking and my headlights firmly off.

I remember, just last week, turning on the light too quickly. Finding you on my recliner. You were bouncing a toddler on your knee, with Dad's eyes and Mum's nose and your impish grin. I flicked the switch before you had a chance to introduce us.

The doctor tells me these are called 'flashbacks'. That I've had a normal, if uncommon, reaction to loss. That there's a wonderful therapist in New Farm who I'll be seeing on Wednesday.

He's right, I know. But I know you too, Michael. I know you're still there, watching, mapping out the world with your pen and your notebook. Invisible until the right colours bring you to life.

I just hope you forgive me.

Pinwheels

Edwina Shaw

On the way into the annual Brisbane show, a stand of rainbow-coloured pinwheels whirred in the wind. I wanted to hold one and blow the petals till they spun but my father shook his head. 'If you get one then your sister and the boys will want one too. We're not made of money.' I wondered what I'd look like if I really was made of money. Purple and blue like five and ten dollar notes with orange twenties for my hair.

My sister and I held my father's hands tight as we fought through the dust and the pushing crowd of belts, handbags and shoes. The boys were with Mummy. I was glad to have Daddy to follow but every time we passed a pinwheel stand I couldn't help looking up at the blurring colours and wishing I could have one. Or a fairy doll on a stick that sprinkled glitter from her dress.

My father dragged us through the agricultural exhibits. 'An educational excursion,' he called it. We had to see everything so we got our money's worth. By the time we rode the chairlift my feet were aching as I swung them back and forth, all the way across to sideshow alley. High above all the displays we'd visited, I clung tight to Daddy's arm. It was a long way down. My hair ribbon came loose and floated, flitting in the wind down and down until I couldn't follow it anymore.

At last we reached the carousel. I smiled and waved at Mummy and my littlest brother every time I went past, craning my head to keep them in sight as long as I could as I rode around and around. But it wasn't my favourite ride. Not really. The best was when Daddy would take both my hands and spin me until I felt as if I'd swirled into a colourful blur—just like the pinwheels.

Later, in the stands, we watched ring events and ate packed sandwiches that had gone soggy, while fireworks lit up the sky. Green! Red! Blue! The cold night-wind stung my cheeks so I burrowed into Daddy's jumper till my nose was warm again.

On the way back to the train station we passed the pinwheels but I knew there was no use asking. And as the train slowly rocked us home I rested my head on my father's lap and wished he would buy us all pinwheels and fairy dolls and strawberry ice creams and five show bags each.

The year my father was dying we didn't go to the show. He couldn't walk from his room to the front door. I didn't feel like going anyway. No one did. We didn't want to face the crowds by ourselves without his hand to hold. It felt like we were pinwheels being blown frantic in the wind, spinning out of control, whirling faster and faster as the pin holding us together rattled, came loose.

Fell away.

Word Search

Beth Clapton

You always knew the strangest things – the name
of the purple flowers which cling to nooks in spring walls
the name of the moon, between half and full, and the part
of your brain which lights up before thought.

What is the word for the thing which propelled me
from my bed to your side in the pre-dawn, what word
sent me searching for the scissors when I saw your
yellowed nails, made me cling to your cooling hand?

I know the word for how we both deferred
to the medicine charts with its columns and rows
to control the morphine. But what's the word
for how my arms ache for the weight of you?

There are words for the colour of sunset
and the carving of hearts on trees,
for the messages in vapour trails in the sky,
but is there a word big enough for this?

Eucalyptus citriodora

Gina Mercer

At the curb, my sister reaches for my hand.
Not expecting it, my hold is awkward, knuckles collide.

She tugs me across the road,
like I'm four again and late for swimming lesson.
Propels me onto the worn,
lion-fur grass beside the church.

We lose momentum
beneath the trunk of a solo
lemon-scented gum, gesturing to the sky
its yearning to escape
the turbid agitation of buses, trucks, cars.

She hands me a handkerchief.

You might need this

My whole 18 year-old body a question.

Mum's been killed

I look at a branch, slender with longing.

Out cycling

She pours out
an inundation of words about
phone calls, times, neighbours,
          police   the Holden responsible.

When she stops
I hand her back the handkerchief.
She's crying.

We hold each other.

There is the crisp *citriodora*
to breathe in
stay with

the way it dances its longing

the way it doesn't collapse.

Lullaby

Eryn Purcell

Dum, da, dum, da . . . dum, dum.

Six piercing beeps sound ascending in a minor key. The tune fills the sterile room every minute or so, bouncing off the four walls, a space devoid of sunlight. Devoid of hope. The melody signifies your life and your death, a musical paradox.

The machine that holds you, the one that beeps, is connected to others. Countless others. I don't know what they all do. But I do know that when they are turned off, and you are stripped of the cords and tubes, that you will live no longer. We must turn them off. It's not fair to keep you here. The finite days of your life have drawn to their inevitable close.

Untangled, you're placed on my chest. Skin to fresh skin. Chest to breast. How my body yearns for you to wake; for this all to have been a mistake. For your heartbeat not to slow and fade but to drum louder than that sterile beeping.

But you don't wake. You slip, pink to pale, away from this world. Calm, content, nestled into my embrace. There is comfort knowing you never suffered but it does not dull the forceful sting of realisation. I will walk away from this place with you in my heart, instead of my arms.

Your Dad cries out, a sound I've never heard him make. It's guttural, frustration and anger bubbling through but, more than that, I can taste his remorse. He would have given his life for yours. So would I.

My tears slow as numbness steals over me. I am silent, absorbing how you feel against my skin, what you smell like as I breathe you in; trying to etch them into my soul so I never forget. This is where I leave you. Where you leave me. And where I leave myself.

And all I can hear are those six beeps. Your life and your death; immortalised in my memory by the NICU lullaby.

Chantelle

Kim Langcake

We still went walking after dinner, the family fanning out behind my father like a jet stream. We had been five before and were five again now. Wandering through the streets as the evenings began to lose their summer shimmer; looking for spitfire grubs on the cooling footpath.

When my sister stepped on a bull-ant she was allowed to scream and carry on like a pork chop. Mum scooped her up with an unfamiliar delicacy and turned for home, the movement and vigour of the small wailing figure at odds with the wan fragility of her rescuer. My brother and I stared in embarrassed confusion at their retreat. Dad finished off the bull-ant with his heel and I thought that his eyes looked like the glittery piece of agate I'd won in a lucky dip at the St John's fete.

My grandparents paid for a holiday on the coast. Dad packed a seasonally inappropriate assortment of clothes for us and forgot to make the customary egg sandwiches for the road. We piled into the Kingswood, whining loudly from the backseat about having to listen to old peoples' music. After a mutinous hour on the road, Dad shifted his three recalcitrant offspring into the back of the wagon and bought fish and chips as a peace offering. Tom Jones sang *Delilah* and Mum watched us silently in the rear view mirror, her endlessly busy hands folded still on her lap.

We went fishing with Dad on the pier every day, learning how to push the hooks through the slimy whitebait and how to gently wriggle our way out of a snag. I said to Dad, 'She gets to keep her name though, doesn't she?' The name had been a collective choice and it seemed important that she got to keep it. Dad told me to cast in again and I watched the line arc through the air, landing with a hopeful splash in the iridescent green. He kissed the top of my head and that felt like an answer.

Mum quietly selected the backseat radio station for us on the way home. I could see her smiling fixedly in the mirror while we sang *Ballroom Blitz* at the tops of our voices.

We went back to our walks after dinner and there were no recurrences of gentle carriage home for insect bites. The days cooled. Dad's eyes lost their gemstone fluidity. The dogged transformation back into five appeared complete.

One night I saw a light on in the room that hadn't yet looped itself back into our lives. I stood at the door and watched as my mother silently folded tiny clothes into plastic bags. Each time a bag was filled she rested her hand on it and closed her eyes. I couldn't tell if she was breathing in or out.

The Last Swim

Alison Jeffries

Over and over I see it
Her last swim
Her tentative step on the sand
Small aqua booties
Small feet
Hair, soft as a baby's
Short tufts, blonde and white
Stolen by chemo
Her *inner-city-trendy* cut we call it
My sister and I
One on each arm
As she enters the water
Step by slow tentative step
It's been a while, she says
And then, the water waist high
She no longer fears the small, incoming waves
She lets go of our arms
And she swims . . .

At first she lies back in the water
Letting its watery fingers caress her body, her head
She floats and gazes at the sky
Lovely, so lovely, she says

Lovely, so lovely, it is
Her beaming face, her eyes half-closed
In those blue-green waters
That perfect cerulean sky . . .

And then she turns over
Treading water, arms making small arcs
We watch her
And remember countless summers
When she watched us from the shore . . .
But now

As the evening sun mottles gold foil on her skin
She turns away from us, lifting her arms
In a strong freestyle stroke
And swims
Away from us
Stronger than us now
Alone, not looking back—
Away from the shore . . .

Under the Sun

Judy Johnson

How many years till I no longer mistake
the tree limb's *screek* outside the window
for your boots' squeaky climb on the stairs
to the front door.

And when will I convince my brain
it has no need to tell the lungs
to hold my breath in wait for your key
that in this life, no longer has a lock.

How many times must I look at the screen
of my ringing phone
expecting your face and name
to be calling.

And at what point will I un-remember
your hands behind my dress
tugging the small, spliced tracks of zip together.
Then gently kissing my neck in gratitude

as though you'd arrived
from a slow journey upwards
on a familiar funicular

my naked back from your window seat
the view you never grew tired of.

How long till the nights
transform from shattering collision
to become the bruises
I know I can bear.

I do not want to heal completely.
To become pristine again like a beach
rehabilitated through no visitors and time.

That would seem as though you had never traversed
the length and breadth of my skin
with your fingers.

Never made a hollow the size and shape of you
out of the warmth of me
to lie down inside and rest
under the sun.

The Space in Between

Kaylia Payne

Daniel died at 3:50pm on 22 October 2015. I learned about it hours later through Facebook. Or, rather, three private messages sent via Facebook in quick succession:

Daniel got into a motorcycle accident.

Police are calling you now.

They say that the crash was fatal.

In books that feature sudden loss, the protagonist usually says, 'I can't remember what happened after that' or 'the rest of the night was a blur.'

If only.

When you learn that someone you love has died suddenly and unexpectedly; when you realise that you'll never see them or speak with them or laugh together again—their future, your future . . . it's all torn to shreds. You fall to the ground, screaming, surrounded by fragments of all the things that will never be.

Donna Tartt writes in her novel *The Secret History,* 'I suppose at one time in my life I might have had any number of stories, but now there is no other. This is the only story I will ever be able to tell.'

I don't have stories anymore. I have A Story: Daniel died. It's the story of my past, present and future, rewriting everything that came before and everything that could have been until there are only those two words left.

Daniel died.

Daniel was my brother. Is my brother. Was my brother? I still don't know which tense to use; people get uncomfortable either way. Which is why, for the most part, I don't talk about him at all.

'We just did an entire course on delivering bad news to families, and then I go and tell you through a fucking Facebook message,' my brother's best friend and fellow medical student said to me during the wake.

Then we laughed, because grief is weird.

In all fairness to him, I didn't do a better job of breaking the news to my parents. Instead, when I called their home phone in Canberra, I began hysterically ranting about motorbikes and Facebook and university pranks and *it can't be real it can't be real it can't be real.*

The sound they made when they finally worked out what I was trying to tell them, the one I play over in my head in the silence of night, is singular proof of the inadequacies of the English language. Words can be a powerful tool for conveying many experiences.

But not this.

Kobayashi Issa, a Japanese haiku master, wrote the following piece after the death of his second son:

This is a dewdrop world.
I know that it is.
and yet . . . and yet . . .

Dewdrops, though beautiful, are transient. As is life. Issa knew that there weren't any words for grief so he let the silence speak instead. The spaces convey his pain far more powerfully than words ever could, and it is in this space that my family and I exist now, both humbled and horrified by the vastness of loss.

References
Issa, K. (1997), The Spring of My Life and Selected Haiku, Translated by S. Hamill, Boston, Shambhala.

Tartt, D. 1992, The Secret History, Random House, New York.

Verandah

Sam Morley

As the sun simmered
my father watched the last light
lap onto the verandah.
He hissed through his cigarette
teeth yellowing in his slack gums.
By then death had reached him.

When he was buried
I just stood there boy-squinting
between men in town hats and tweed
who were mute when words
may have made flesh a memory
now only sashed in smoke.

The Old-Fashioned Habit

Dani Glatz

He always carries a hanky
'Man-sized'
Dad sized
Ironed and folded
And well-worn like him

The old-fashioned habit of a gentle man

And as men who are gentle do
He gave me his hanky
At her funeral
Somewhere to put my tears
Whilst keeping his own inside

Kindness

Linda Harding

She was so tender with you, that nurse in the ICU, talking to you as she moved you on the bed, adjusting the wires and tubes around your comatose little body. 'Sorry sweetheart,' she would say, 'I just have to move this here. There you are darling, that's better.' Her movements were gentle, soft, achingly sensitive to our love for you.

She was doing things for you I could not do. She was making you more comfortable on your journey away from life. She was making sure that you were cherished till the end.

It's what I remember now after all these years; her profound kindness.

There were other kind people that day: the paramedics, the strangers on the beach who cared for your brothers, orderlies and cleaners at the hospital, friends who sat with us and prayed. There was the young doctor who had to tell us there was no hope left and you would die at only four years old. His eyes were full of tears. They were tears for us and for himself. He had poured out his days and nights learning how to save yet here he faced a terrible impotence. He could not save you. No one could save you.

They had tried so hard; pushed air into your drenched lungs, pressed firmly into your chest to make your heart pump, injected drugs to help you live, to no avail. You were going to die and somehow, we who loved you, had now to navigate waters so deep they threatened to drown us, too.

We were on a sacred voyage of grief and needed the kindness. They all knew it. Deep in shock, barely aware of our own bodies, let alone our surroundings, we still managed to register the compassion; a beacon in the fog.

You see, my darling, I have blocked out the beeps and buzzes from the ICU and my memory is hazy as to where we were sitting in that ward in those final moments, holding your small, limp body one last time. But the tenderness, the soft, loving words from that nurse towards you, my dear, well that memory is still crystal clear.

You were, to the end, a small and loved person to her. She mirrored my understanding of you, affirmed your worth. Conscious or unconscious, living or quietly dying, you were always your darling self, our delight, precious beyond all imagining. Her actions said 'Amen' to all of that.

The truth is, little one, that even after the brutal shock of your death, after all the years of agonising grief, after our own inner deaths and resurrections, kindness, like love, still wins. It always wins.

Key Change

Fiona Lynch

You, c-shaped, ankles crossed under a piano stool,
suspended notes, pages the colour of weak tea, cases
buckled, black and stiff. Rememberings—the kitchen

sink, his arms around your thighs, deckled light
in the story chair, bedtime kisses to his forehead,
sheets printed with blue planes, you tippy-toeing

back to the lounge, the warm belly of a mug of tea,
him dreaming. Grief watches your folded songs,
cups your shoulder, taps the metronome *You are deaf*

to the tone of Spring, freesias farewelled the bones
of winter, Sunday smells like sluiced grass.
Through the lounge sash, a wren flits, her morning

bath. Your fingers hover on ivory, chin tilting, lifting,
lids closed. An aria splashes out—bare feet on baltic
boards, teddy and him in your bed. You held him

in your nape, stroked away his monsters, sang his lashes
dry. You played the melody of him, reached every octave.
His name is a whole note, with fermata, a whole note.

Always the Music

Jackie Tritt

It was music that got you through the bad days. And the good. Always.

At first, I sang to calm you when your tiny feet stretched the skin on my belly and, once you were born, whenever you were restless.

We sang at kindergarten and made simple instruments to shake and bang. And as you grew a little older you designed your own instruments.

There were the bagpipes you made from the discarded bladder of a wine cask, with a straw in one end and a tin whistle in the other. You nearly passed out from the alcoholic fumes.

The flat-faced fiddle. Almost a fiddle but not quite.

The real fiddle you started to make on Year 10 work experience. You studied Strobel's book on violin making. You absorbed delightful new words and techniques: purfling, bee sting, chamfer, volute. And after all that hard work, your completed violin sounded great.

And, constantly, you listened to music. Listened over and over until every note, every nuance, had sunk into your fingers. Until the notes would pour out from you, effortlessly: Irish, Brazilian, Appalachian, jazz. Once heard, never forgotten. On almost any instrument—from mandolin to violin to balalaika; from penny whistle to flute and ocarina. From keyboard to djembe.

And with the music came the joy and ongoing friendships of musicians in each band which formed and, in time, dissolved. And always bliss on your face as the music took over.

And when you yellowed and sickened; when cancer and pain crept through your body, you naturally turned to music for solace. Friends arrived week after week bearing instruments and memories. Celtic friends, bluegrass friends, jazz friends, uni friends. Each transported you to another time, another place. Each took you to another level where there was no pain and a beatific smile spread across your face.

Even in palliative care you asked us to bring in your gear so you could work on your last cd, on the final mix and edit. Your good friend Lance had taken you to the forest so you could record your latest, your last, tune—*Forest*. You played it on tin whistle. Just those plaintive notes and, in the background, chirping birds and the *shush-shush* of creek water over boulders.

It was Lance who MC'd your funeral. In the forest, exactly as you'd planned together. You'd have loved it. So much joyful music, so many friends and rellies clapping along, and your three kids playing tunes you'd worked on together. Even the *Last Post* on kazoo. Your final musical joke.

And to finish, Lionel, your friend forever, played *Forest* on tin whistle. Silence. Just the birds. Leaves fluttering from tall trees, golden in the winter sunlight. You centre stage in your coffin. Our tears streaming.

Your dad listens to your final cd, over and over. It connects him to you.

I can't stay in the same room. It distresses me too much. Grieving, I've found, sways to many different tunes.

After

Janet Lee

We are in the store and the salesman is showing us ones with French doors and ice dispensers and talking of crisper drawers like they matter.

We are buying a new fridge.

You ask me if we bought our current fridge *that* year?

I say yes.

I don't say anything else.

I am thinking of our fridge. I am thinking of that year. I am thinking of her being born. I can see myself putting the breast milk in the freezer, in little bottles with white lids and a place for the date. We bought them specially.

Our freezer has just that one ice cube tray, the one where you turn the handle and the cubes fall into a tray underneath. They aren't cubes; they are rectangles. I am not sure what you call them when they are not square cubes. Suddenly, this matters.

I was gushing then, *churning it out like a jersey cow*, you said.

You laughed when I used the cabbage leaves in my bra but bought them for me anyway and the chooks ate them afterwards.

We were glad of that frozen milk—when I took the antibiotics—and our baby was allergic. We fed her that milk from the freezer.

I pumped, and tipped my fresh milk down the sink.

Tainted.

Later, when I was off the antibiotics, I would feed her and then store the rest, build up the freezer stash, just in case the mastitis came back.

It did.

After.

In the stillness of After, I remember my mother taking the clothes and nappies away.

Just like they had taken her.

But not to the same place.

I remember my mother packing things away, tidying things up, wiping things clean.

Taking the memories somewhere else.

I looked, but did not see.

Because it was After.

Months later, when I had taken out the last of the cooked meals and was hunting for dinner among the frozen meat and ice-cream, I found it, one tiny bottle with a white lid and a date.

Bought specially.

We have had our fridge twelve years, I say.

Long time, the salesman says.

You look at me.

No, I say, not really.

Update on Lulu

Linda Godfrey

Lulu eats edamame for breakfast while she reads the paper and drinks black tea. She doesn't listen to the radio. She gets lost in its shallows when she is looking for space.

Lulu buys coloured clothes online but only wears black pants and singlets. It's the one colour that holds her frame of mind.

Lulu was told that her father couldn't die until he had spoken to her, but she didn't believe the messenger.

Lulu dreams of phones ringing in the middle of the night but can't find hers. Waiting on the ring, dreading the ring.

Who knew after watching all those tv programs where people fall down, instantly dead, that death is a drawn out process of slowly shutting down. What a thing, such a thing.

They say death comes in threes. It was a race to the end between Tao and Dad. Who will be the third? Maybe a noisy miner, maybe a lorikeet, wasn't there a spotted dove recently? Let's count that and be done.

Lulu is an orphan. A hoarder of bones and ash, a hoarder of secrets.

Lulu has a big tree in her backyard. It drops widow-maker branches. It has crushed two clotheslines this summer. It's home to a family of ravens.

Lulu finds the heads of doves and pieces of rat skin in the birdbath. The ravens are soaking and softening them to eat later.

Lulu loves driving long distances on her own. She can cry freely and curse and shout at big utes racing past speeding.

Lulu has a restless body, spilling over the edges of her bed. With the sound of crashing waves at night she dreams of coffins falling over. A friend says it's whales breaching out at sea.

The most interesting things to Lulu are limits. Can a white string make the outline of a grave, or do you need a spray painted line in yellow neon? Can you have both? Lulu wants both.

In the long run

Marjorie Lewis-Jones

And I think of you sprinting. Just a minute or two. Never seen you do it. But I know you did it then. One hundred metres before dawn. No ambulance at the station at the end of your sprint. It was out saving someone else. (Someone else's wife?) You forever thinking: I should have called. Sprinting back home. Giving her mouth-to-mouth. Between breaths begging for resurrection. She had fallen. She was felled. Stepping away from the home ventilator—or maybe *to it.* I never knew. She gasped. A thud. Body to floor. You called out (naturally). 'Okay?' No answer. Out of bed. Kneeling by her side. She was out cold in the hall. Or in the kitchen. Or in the dining room. I don't know. I should know. I never asked. Can't now. Nobody knows now you're gone. She was your lodestar—and her light went out—and you stumbled. Kept going. Staggered. Tried not to let it ruin you. Didn't shift a thing she'd shoved into cupboards after the move. 'Later,' she'd said. 'I'll do it later.' But then had no *later* to do it in. All dreams and drudgery un-done. *Dearest.* I saw this written in cards from you to her. That era of gentleman. A gentle man. *Dearest.* A delicate word. Like violets. Like roses. Leads me to her dressing table with the wing mirrors. Multiple selves applying a comet of claret-hued lipstick (her only shade). And her there *then.* Not now. Her absence. Takes it out of me still. Whips my breath away. Bends me double like a stitch.

It took me years not to think of her when I ran.

Small Steps

Hannah Trott

I looked at my dress hanging on the door and figured I'd better feed the dog before I put it on, don't wanna get it dirty. Then I scolded myself for being so fucking stupid. As if a muddy paw print matters at a time like this. Just get dressed.

With trembling hands I did all 17 tiny buttons up, brushed out my hair and debated over putting on lipstick. Don't want to look too put together or people will think I'm not grieving properly, don't want to look too dishevelled either, I'm talking at this thing after all. God, why do I even care what people think?

I came out of the bedroom and looked at my partner sitting at the kitchen table like any other morning. He looked up at me, 'ready?' Just get to the car.

He tried to make light conversation, I knew he was trying to take my mind off of what was to come but, fucking hell, would he just shut up already. I turned the radio up even though I didn't know the song and frankly, did not care for it. I saw him look at me and I felt bad for making his life harder when he was trying so hard.

I walked to my seat at the front of the church reserved for me. 500 pairs of eyes were on me as I walked down the aisle, I didn't recognise any of them apart from weirdly, at the last second, my high school maths teacher. I shook my head. Just get to the chair.

I sat through the Pastor's droning sermon and thought about how he would've hated this. I remembered how once when he was in high school and drunk at a party, he had actually punched the Pastor's son. I smiled to myself and wondered if he knew.

Then I was being called up to deliver a eulogy. I looked at the three full pages with their size twelve font and wished I hadn't worn such uncomfortable heels. Just read the thing.

I looked at my dad, I looked at my nan, I looked at my high school maths teacher whose name I still can't remember and I looked at the coffin in front of me and thought again how he would've hated white lilies. Who chooses white lilies for a 20 year old boy?

I read the eulogy. I followed the coffin out of the church. I watched as it was lowered into the earth and I wandered around the golf club for an hour while people came up to me and said 'I'm so sorry about your brother' and passed me mini quiches.

Just gotta get through the rest of my life.

Goodness

Chloe Warren

In November, I awoke with an aching throat from the bushfire smoke.

Emerging from my air-conditioned office block into the haze one afternoon, I remember peeling a plastic sticker from an apple and acknowledging, 'The world would be cleaner if I did not exist.'

I didn't know what to do with my body at night. We had nowhere to put the unrest; we continued our lives as normal while our country burned and others disappeared under water. What were we to do?

In December, I flew back to England. My grandfather had been suddenly hospitalised, and he died ten days later.

We grieved for the loss of him at the same time as trying to piece together a new semblance of normality for my grandmother, whose Alzheimer's had already begun to erode her memories, identity, and resilience. Each evening, we watched the news of the fires at home and I couldn't tell where any of the pain came from anymore. My world had fallen apart. The world was falling apart.

We took it in turns to cope, each waiting our turn to collapse under the weight of what we had lost.

Being in London before my flight home, the city's inescapable juxtaposition of privilege and poverty was a constant ringing in my ears. How did this become normal? I caught the eye of a homeless man through a window as I perched on a stool in a busy cafe, and for a second his image aligned with the reflection of my diamond ring in the glass.

My dad had given me cash for Christmas—a tradition, he called it 'ice cream money'—and that evening on the way back to my AirBnB I gave £10 and £20 notes to people sleeping in shop doorways. I just wanted to feel good.

It was a selfish goodness.

It was a hopeless goodness.

The cost of my ability to hold my grandfather's hand as he died equated to more than five tonnes of carbon. That was what love had cost. Each time I unwrapped the plastic around my in-flight meals, I cringed.

Returning home, some days I could bring myself to face old normalities, and it would feel like end of the emptiness. Each time the emptiness came back, it was as though those periods of functionality had been delusional. That to be functional was to lie.

I don't know how much of this realisation came down to grief.

I thought grief would feel like sadness, like missing a person, adjusting to an absence.

It feels less like an absence and more as though the shape of everything has changed.

Because it changed, I don't know where I fit. I cannot adjust to normality because it has gone. Its home has been emptied of furniture and I cannot go back there again.

Then the pandemic happened.

And I am no longer alone in my grief.

Fire Once Applied to Feathers

Jessica Valvasori

I read about the dead birds of the Australian bushfires and my stomach hurls with bilious acid. Images of our native birds, captured so mercilessly, half-exposed in burnt-wet ash: the hunted, charcoaled victims of fire country.

The violation of colour nauseates me: blue-black, yellow-black, red-black, green-purple-black. Rosella-black. Honeyeater-black. Yellow-tailed-black. King-Parrot-black. *Black-black.* Colours the human eye should never see. I am reminded of colour mixing tip number 8: *Always add dark to light.* But did anyone ever imagine there could be so much dark?

I picture the images hung in a gallery, suffocating its own white walls, accompanied by a small, elegant tombstone: *the unpalatable hues of fire once applied to feathers.* And beneath each image, a brass eulogy to death:

Rainbow Lorikeet.

Possibly a Honeyeater.

A Juvenile Crimson Rosella.

Unidentifiable Parrot.

Possibly a Red-tailed Black-Cockatoo.

Species Unknown.

Species Unknown.

I stare vacantly at the lifeless wet piles of birds, feeling an overwhelming need to witness. Sand clings to black shapes, smothering flight. Smothering beauty and identity. In a single colourless photograph, the Mallacoota birds lie butterflied along the beach. A string of incongruous debris: unbelonging to the land. These washed-up angels of fire.

I follow the page, noticing other text, grasping only snippets: *'tide of ash . . . extinction event . . .'* And the words that do break through, *'100 dead birds . . . 25 species . . . '* infiltrate me with the brutal finality of a fire-ravaged death. *'Unimaginable scenes of carnage.'*

I think of the men and women who removed burnt carcasses from charred fence lines. *Black-black.*

Is there a name for the colour of burnt-out eye sockets?

Possibly a King-Parrot-black.

The colours blur on the page. Mix to nothingness.

Massacre-black.

A final helpless thought: can we ever unsee that which we have seen?

How to Make Sage Butter

Chloe Brien

Serves 1

Pick a small handful of sage from the garden you grew
as a reminder that some things can never be tamed. Tear up the sage
with shaking hands.

In a medium pan, add torn sage to one tablespoon unsalted butter.

Stir slowly with a wooden spoon. Try not to burn
the butter, but if you do let it show how
life doesn't always go to plan.

Season, then heat until the sage becomes fragrant.

Let the perfumed oil reach your nose, bringing back
that night a cortège of you lit a smoking brand
in the room where she died, smudging the air
to show her the way home.

Feel the sting of tears and put down the spoon.

Question why you're allowed to live when she isn't
despite everything she offered that you have not.

Remember when you howled through whiskey
the day you knew she was gone.

The way each moment takes the hurt further out
to sea, though the tide will often bring it back.

Pick up the spoon again and stir.

Remember that even if the world didn't let her live, you are
alive, impossibly, like a whistle through the teeth in a high wind.

Enjoy with your pasta of choice.

Someone Put the Kettle On

Jean Kearney

In her final week, I almost didn't drive up. There had been so many moments I had thought would be the last goodbye—when she was still standing, still talking, still conscious. Goodbyes that would have left me sad, but at a distance. Sadness divorced from place. Free to disperse.

But Ruth was already there, alone with her family. And so I drove those six hours, along deserted, half paved roads, not knowing if I should be rushing.

When I finally arrived, the farm looked unchanged. Exactly as it appeared in the sun-weathered photos salvaged from long forgotten albums. Except that the tennis court was now overgrown and spluttering with catheads. The rocking chair coated with dust and rusted, disappearing into the unkempt garden. The porch, empty.

I could feel the weight of memory that hung around the place. Ever present, but not alive. Heaving everyone closer to the past. Nothing separated the days or the years.

Here, deafness and dementia were at home.

On her last afternoon, we moved her metal-frame hospital bed into the centre of the lounge, where we usually passed 40°C days watching *Midsomer Murders* and blasting Louis Armstrong. The great-grandchildren had been driven off 10 minutes earlier, and there was no hum of energy to fend off the hoarse breaths. I sat deep in an armchair, slightly removed, and quietly sketching—a shield to observe this most private moment—to know where to be.

The grandfather entered, deaf to earlier, urgent calls. His rickety, sun scarred legs unstably carried him, hands reaching continuously for the support of chairs and tables. He sank down beside her, and beside Ruth. The two of them, touching her, touching each other.

Time wavered as we waited, and I drew four sketches. One daughter at the foot of the bed. One at the side. Her body enveloped by blankets. Hands.

Out of the silence, Uncle Marty, with his great swollen legs propped up, spoke suddenly.

'It's going to be 41 degrees tomorrow!'

'Did you hear that mum? 41 degrees! You're not missing anything!'

But she was already gone.

It hung in the air. And we waited. Ill-equipped to judge whether someone was no more.

Her body rested weightlessly amongst the sheets and pillows. We hovered aimlessly, waiting for the doctor to arrive. Waiting for closure, the grandfather tried to close her mouth, forcibly, to preserve her dignity.

When the doctor came, and pronounced her dead, he was unable to close one of her eyes. She was covered.

Two men from the funeral home arrived—country men, shedding their high-vis shirts and khaki shorts, wearing ill-fitting suits. Out of respect. The suits clung and hung simultaneously. They carefully raised her body off the bed and into a bag, a van, a coffin, fire.

She was gone, and still everyone was waiting. There was no full stop.

Instead, the night wearing on, someone put the kettle on.

Phone-calls and Waterfalls

Anthony Williamson

I'm oceans away when she calls.
She sounds adrift, I*t's come out of the blue, MS and cancer.*
Her words pound into me like roaring breakers.
Stage four... nodes... aggressive... untreatable...
I steal a breath and splutter out platitudes, *Sis, everything will be fine. Really.*
The kids, she whispers and swallows.

I recall a lifetime earlier, when we were small,
She fell so ill that my father had to drive her to hospital.
They kept her in Intensive Care for days, but I steadfastly refused to visit.
If she couldn't say goodbye to me, I knew she'd have to come home.
And I was proudly right.

I phone each week to be there.
She tries everything, suffers more.
It even submerges for a while before bursting out and drenching her.
I'm so bloody helpless, she sobs one night,
The kids though, they're being great. Washing me, wiping me.
She breaks down again. I try and lift her up, *Hey, so you try a new treatment-*
False hope, I hear her partner growl darkly in the background.
My chest heaves, I know how much he loves her.
No, no more treatment, she says, *We want to make the most of it.*
Somewhere a little boy clenches his fists.

A month later the phone wrenches me from bad dreams. I'm soaked.
I'm sorry, she's going. She's in a lot of pain but wants to say goodbye. Be quick.
I urgently wipe at my face to collect my thoughts but the little boy blocks me.

He shoves me away from what I need to say. I strain to talk over him,
Sis, you're so amazing, so brave.
Your life, you impacted so many people, your wisdom, kids-
A hard voice cracks through the phone,
You're confusing her. Just say goodbye.
My mind goes blank.
Then I see the little girl getting home, running to the little boy, smiling.
I grab his flailing arms and pull him in tight.
He slows and finally collapses into me.
My heart flows through my words,
I love you. It's okay. I love you.
There's a pause then my sister speaks heavily and slowly and slurred,
I love you.
I hear pride. I smile through my tears and nod and sob.
And ever so gently, we let her go.

Moments

Kelli Hawkins

When you died, I was relieved.

I couldn't tell anyone that of course. What would they think? Relieved my husband was dead.

I couldn't tell them how it felt watching cancer take over your body. Watching it infect your blood. Your bones. Even your mind. I hated so much about you being sick. I hated it when the nurses came to wash you. I'd hover, protective but useless. *It hurts him to move,* I'd say, the words not conveying the horror of your pain. I'd hope they'd put it off. Sometimes they did. But it *had to be done.* By the end five nurses were needed. Painkillers first. A needle; stronger drugs almost every day. One held your head, two others each side. Then three, two, one. They'd push or pull you with sheets or hands. You'd cry out, even if sleeping, your face stretched, mouth wide as your body twisted. Sometimes I could see they regretted it. *Sorry, I'm sorry, we'll be quick* they'd say as they wiped a cloth down your protruding spine or under a bony arm. I'd move around the bed as they worked, staying in your line of sight, even if those eyes were screwed shut, murmuring *I'm here, I'm here, nearly done.* Sheets yanked off, slipped back on, tucking in hospital corners as you panted and I sweated, the dread an ever-present nausea deep in my stomach. *Hurry up,* I'd think. *Finish what you started.* Then, *done.* Finally. With visible relief they'd say *it's over now.* If you were still conscious, you'd nod, try for a smile. A *smile.* Your grace was more than I could stand. You were dying, your spine broken and they tugged at you in the name of cleanliness. They meant well, but the *pain.* Then, you'd glance at me with pleading eyes. Beads of sweat. I'd say *he needs more.* They'd nod, not arguing. The search for unbruised skin. Another needle. Moans and cries until you slipped back into the darkness.

Pain. One of a thousand moments of pain for me to remember.

But I don't want to remember. I want to forget your pain. I want to remember the brilliant years of blissful ignorance that slipped merrily past us before you got sick. You chasing the children down the hall as they shrieked with laughter. Bodysurfing in the ocean. Drinking wine in the winter sun on the back deck. Sitting together on the couch or at the movies or in the car. Hellos at the airport. Thousands of moments of fun.

Of love.

Why can't I remember those moments?

So, I can't tell them I'm relieved. Relieved our children don't see you only in hospital after school, attached to machines, bruised but somehow still smiling. Relieved you are no longer in pain. That I don't have to watch that pain, be responsible for it, beg the nurses and doctors to stop it, *please.*

I could tell them, I guess.

But I don't want to upset them.

7 White - 1976

John O'Callaghan

There was complete silence as he appeared suddenly in the glass pane outside our door. We 36 became one in the absolute silence; inside the terror now familiar inside this classroom. Our fear felt like a burning fire inside a building one cannot get out of.

Outside this room, our mothers hung washing out and our fathers were busy in their offices, yet our fathers knew what was about to happen, for they had each been here decades earlier. Our arms were folded on old desks. We sat up perfectly straight & still.

He marched in, shining black shoes, crisp white dress with black cord holding together his strange uniform from another century. Brother Cassian Blackwood was the most frightening man we would ever meet in our lives.

He still hadn't said a word. He was scanning the silent room looking for someone to attack, assault, fling against his blackboard and we all knew this. We were 12 years old. I sat terrified, trying not to be; trying not to be noticed; trying to feign invisibility, yet, I and all of us knew we were trapped for the next 40 minutes which felt like hours.

On this particular morning, he picked out Nick, a tough kid with big, tougher brothers at Hamilton Marist Brothers, from a large Catholic family. We didn't notice or hear anything which Nick did to attract the radar of Cassian; but then one didn't actually have to do anything.

Nick, alarmingly, decided to stand up to Cassian. We do not know if this had ever happened before in this room down the decades. Nick stood his ground in the aisle, hands on his hips in his blue shirt, blue & gold tie, grey trousers—our new uniform we were proud of.

Br Cassian, the man of unlimited power in this room, the punisher of a thousand boys before us, stepped down off the platform and made his way slowly towards Nick who did not move. All of us were now extremely worried because we could not protect Nick; it was everyone surviving alone in here.

Cassian began punching into Nick who had sinned by failing to show fear. He was punching with his old white knuckles. I was only two feet away and I could hear Nick's ribcage echoing. He punched him probably a dozen times and Nick didn't flinch. We were spellbound and this is how it was—no one made a sound. Nick had actually won.

This was our 1970s reality. All of us were there to learn about fear, it was meant to be a religion lesson but we were learning to just to survive, to blend in and never stick out, otherwise risk getting thrashed by a man who long ago seemed to have lost his humanity.

While Nick was being attacked, I looked at the wooden pencil case on my desk. It looked like a replica of a coffin and I only wanted to slide the lid open and lie down inside it and go to sleep. Some of us didn't survive that place; some of us did die.

Nick died at 21 and I, who was the opposite of Nick, somehow survived, I have no idea how. I never told Mum & Dad; none of us did. It was our normal, which was so abnormal. I saw Cassian twenty years or so later, at a proud Marist Centenary dinner. None of my class mates went near him, he was the only one there in uniform. He was exactly the same. I spoke to him briefly but not the words I wanted to speak.

Your Call to Heal

Susan Tattersall

My sense of loss is multitudinous, fractured, jarring and palpable, with me right now. It comes from the loss of you and the loss of myself.

My grief for you was as expected as your death. We shared a rare mother daughter bond and friendship, our nightly calls started almost 40 years ago when I was training to be a police officer and we spent time together as much as we could.

In the weeks before you took your last breath, I stayed with you, first in the spare room and then in a single bed tucked between the wall and your queen. On our last night together, we held hands and you later slipped out of your room without me waking for the first time, for the very last time.

You were pale in your chair, in the corner of your lounge of over 45 years when I rose that morning. No breath to cause the rise and fall of your chest, and pale, but serene and peaceful.

In the months after you died, I worked through my thoughts with pages of words. I wrote of our love and friendship, our years together and how proud and honoured I was to be your daughter and friend, and still am.

After a while, my thoughts and my writing changed. It was as if a chasm had opened and was being filled with unwanted policing memories. And then one cool morning with the sun emerging out of the darkness and the air crisp, I wrote, 'I think I've finally got it. While you were alive, my demons were kept at bay. Now I can't talk with you, they are unleashed!'

Once unleashed, memories of horrendous happenings jumped from my throat, pulling with them sobs and the raw emotions I had buried deep. I was being turned inside out and backwards as recollections and physical sensations invaded my waking and dreaming.

Twisted and defenceless, the recognition I was grieving for who I once was prior to witnessing trauma wrapped is tentacles around me. My well-cultivated poker face was falling layer after layer as memories of incident after incident added to the very first shock and grief felt as a first responder to a six year old angel departed on tarmac.

You knew the effect of what I'd seen, heard, smelt and felt while a policewoman, particularly the infamous clergyman and my response to bush smoke. I'm sure you sensed my brokenness over those last few years and I am sure you are with me now, guiding me to finally unravel myself and heal. I have felt your wings Mum, you shushing my despair and your eternal guiding wisdom since you left our world.

Although I miss you terribly, I am at peace with your passing. Our relationship was a gift I will always cherish and I now cherish the opportunity to return to you the most important gift possible, reclaiming your girl from under the blue mask of trauma. In your honour.

Vessels

Scott-Patrick Mitchell

We'd coax pattern with a prayer, conjure sky into tank.
At dawn, I'd bring water into a cool room: morning was a ritual, you.
We gathered as if this were a place of work, because all family is labour,
needs constant tending.
Unconditional, our love was service at kitchen's altar.
We piled pills as sacrament: vitamins in my palm, medication in yours.
You always drank first from the jug, my handprint engulfing the fade
of yours: how whorls blessed and pressed us into us.
The topography of your skin stretched through a century.
How those age spots were not there when you first baptised me beneath
the current of your lungs. I was thirsty for tidal worship, the torrent of
tales you regaled, spilling from you, liminal, quavering between here
and the next place.
Your life was a spirit you gave away in fragments and fables, as if
anecdotes were an antidote to disappearance.
            I learnt that I cannot hold on to a river, a creek.
                        My liturgy was an eventuality. It collected at
                the edge of thirst's lip.   Drowned all land
                we had salvaged, in this house built.
I could hear the vibration of how you would end. After days of listening
to it approach, encroach, I was exhaustion. That night, I released brine
from my eyes, turned sheets white with salt lake. This was preparation.
        Now that you are gone, every morning I rehydrate, check in
    with myself, make sure I don't ache. Too much. Listen to sea, revel
    in the bloom of spume: you are remembered, a shell to the ear,
    whispering.
Outside, I ask rain to come, hide me from death in the skirt of it. I
know that in the cycle of such things that the weather brings,
                        a drought shall
                                    follow. And when it does,
                            it will be the memory of us
                                    this mist hollows, how the
                            bowl of our bodies become
                                                coracle,
                                    vessels that ferry us on.

The Story of Us

Megan Brown

You could say I fell for him the first time I met him, talked to him, brushed my hand against his, and kissed him. Our lips met in that initial moment quickly, and so softly that I could barely feel it. The aftermath that short kiss had on my heart was like nothing I had ever felt before.

It was pure bliss and pure magic.

People say it's hard to find a person who does that to you. That gets you. Who leaves such an imprint on your heart it hurts to even think of them.

The moment I met him, he ruled and owned my heart. I was truly and unconditionally his.

Now all I feel is his absence.

I felt like I lost him even before he left this earth.

The man I loved deeply and truly had been wandering in the shadows for some time. But now the shadows had absorbed him whole. Leaving behind beautiful memories that would make me weep. Because I knew there was no way we could be together until it was my turn to leave this earth.

It felt like moments ago that he was alive. Yet, he had already been gone. Lost within himself and his own mind that it felt like he didn't even exist anymore. Like he was dead, before being declared dead.

That's what I had feared the most—the phone call no one wants to hear. The phone call that would shatter my heart more than anything else.

I felt like I had lost a part of myself.

Left numb and fighting to stay afloat. As I finally received that shattering phone call, silent tears streamed down my face as my mind absorbed the news.

He did what he thought was best, his note had read. He wanted me to know that he was trying to protect me. He still loved me, though, and his decision was not what he wanted but what he believed he had to do.

He had to end things because the future he once imagined with me was now replaced with pain and nothing else. That's the sad part about the whole situation. He saw a not so bright future for himself and could not see beyond that image. Believe me, I tried to convince him things would get better but he didn't listen.

It made me weep at how low his heart had sunk; how far gone his beautiful mind had gotten.

It had frightened me when we walked the same earth, that one day our paths would split. Then I would no longer have him by my side.

Now I must walk the path alone, until we meet again.

Previous editions of
Grieve
are available to purchase as
paperbacks or downloadable ebooks from
grieveproject.org

The death of walking

Rachael Mead

This time last year, life was all about feet.
Size eleven, bunions, footprints like continents.
In summer rain, the Roman cobbles were kryptonite.

The delight of strolling from the Spanish Steps to the alleys
of Aventino, my stride threaded with stress after scattering
self-respect in the gutter outside the Baths of Caracalla.

To be alone in Rome was a *pas de deux* of wonder and worry.
My eyes owned the city, but travel by anything but foot
was the province of knotted gut. Trains, departure boards,

pickpockets. Transfers to tiny and tinier stations. Buses
and tickets then trundling my suitcase into the hamlet
at the foot of the Alps. At last and again, it was all about feet.

Every day sunshine and grasslands boiling with colour and cowbells.
Hiking boots better known than my toes, I marched those hills
for a month, my limp sounding the valleys to a private beat.

Today, these ugg boots whiff of wet fur but the couch is bare.
My heart slugs indigo inside my ribs. Time is thinner here.
A place where even soft things break. There's no reason to walk.

The pace of my days no longer thumps to tailbeat or wet-nosed
pleas for scent-snuffle or messages left on bark. The leash hangs
by the door. The outside is a fable I once believed. Days pass

glazed in hooks. Boots gather dust and the fruit bowl grows fur.
Weak light slides in but the beds of sun lie empty. This ache is fractal,
hollowness blooming boundless hollows. Beyond the glass, the world fills

its spaces with sound but in here everything is shadow and silence,
ears tuned for the jingling of tags that does not come. I tuck away
my feet. Beside me, the empty seat stretches itself, quiet and cold.

Look At You

Camille McBride

You open the curtains and I groan, burrowing deeper under the covers. I imagine you grinning, pretending to be oblivious to my hangover. I must forgive you, because you have brought me treats. You offer the tart and coffee as you get into bed, scooting me up for space. I haven't seen you in months and I feel guilty at having spent so much time with my friends during this visit. I think of you alone at home with two small boys while he works nightshift—even when he's home, he's out back with his mates . . .

'Drinks tonight? He said it's okay . . . ' Your big hopeful brown eyes search mine.

Look at you. Even with your hair in a messy half-bun and your clothes dishevelled and mismatched, you look beautiful. You take a drag of your cigarette and exhale slowly, a small smirk playing on your lips. It occurs to me you have already planned it all, you probably know what you will wear and where we will go. You know I won't say no because we both know I've been neglecting you.

I smile and nod as I savour the taste of my favourite tart. I realise I don't know anyone else who will serve me dessert for breakfast.

Look at you. I see the glances as you stride in. The barflies hover and I watch them jostle for your attention. You are polite so I think you enjoy it—maybe even need it right now, these unoriginal men with their unoriginal lines. By the time you're ready to leave, you are glowing. As you drive, I notice the faded bruise on your forearm, but I know better than to ask about it again. Why don't you just leave him, I once asked, and you smiled sadly at my naiveté.

We say goodbye at the airport, and I hug you fiercely. Your hair smells sweet with a hint of cigarettes. I see the fresh bruise and my searching eyes find yours, but you look away. I don't want to change the subtle balance in this morning's mood; I'm a coward like that. You are stubborn and stoic, and I'm not confident enough. Your long nails tickle my arm and I look up.

'I've ordered your birthday present and it'll be here next time.' Your eyes plead and I nod. I turn to leave, my bag as heavy as my heart with all the baked goods you have sent me home with.

The next time I see you is at the morgue. Your long black hair is in sharp contrast to the metal table you're lying on, and your bandaged midriff is the only thing that alludes to your fate. I squeeze you gently, not sure if this is morgue-protocol, but I don't care. He stopped you from leaving—just like you said he would. I am transfixed and numb. I look at you one long, last time. I am lost without you.

More than a Number

Lydia C. Lee

The death toll kept rising but we congratulated ourselves on 'flattening the curve'.

We light-heartedly mocked the Government for their mishandling of the *Ruby Princess* while casually remarking on our good fortune that the hospitals hadn't been overrun. The figures weren't too bad.

We were doing our bit.

We looked at the charts. So many charts.

We checked the numbers, the percentages, and importantly, the recoveries.

It was just a new way of life for a bit. But it was life all the same.

Until it wasn't.

A phone call.

It always starts with a phone call.

It wasn't a number. It was Dad.

In this strange world the unthinkable seemed beyond comprehension.

How did this happen to us? This isn't how it happens in real life. The conversations flowed confusingly over me. I heard words in a disjointed riddle. A puzzle I had no interest in solving.

The details I wanted to know but couldn't bear to hear.

We couldn't have a funeral. Not a proper one.

Mum still had to isolate. She couldn't come.

We sat in the church spaced out. No one to hug you. Our kids couldn't come because of numbers. Always talk of numbers.

No friends, no neighbours.

I felt alone in my grief. I was alone.

It's an icy desolation. A hollowness swelling from the inside.

I sat in my car. There was no sharing of stories. No reflecting on happy times. No long lost faces to pay respects. No celebration of the life that had touched so many others, as long lives do. This was a microscopic version of a man who meant so much to us for so long. There is comfort offered in the expansive shared mourning at a funeral. It was missing. This funeral was small. Not intimate, diminished. Despoiled.

Time passes but nothing changes. Every morning I hear the numbers. These numbers. These words we are familiar with as an abstract idea. Not abstract for me. A searing ache that demands attention. I'm stuck. I'm angry at the numbers, at the callous statistics.

I cry wondering who lost a parent or partner. I mourn for them, thinking of their lonely farewells. I want to know the details of 'who'. Who are these numbers? Who did they leave behind? Who can't get comforted? Who also sits in a small room with four walls growing bigger with each hour looming? Who can't concentrate because they're angry? Who can't function because they're numb? Who are these numbers?

Who went into this 'new normal' and discovered their life changed forever?

Who?

Me.

Grieving for my home in Africa

Sagamba Muhira and James Page

Africans love traditional sayings, and one popular saying is: 'When elephants fight, the grass gets flattened'. Elephants are huge creatures, common to Africa, and often they fight. I have seen grass which has been crushed flat after a fight between elephants. This is a useful summary of the experience of war in my home country. The elephants in this case were the nations that fought in my country, and the grass crushed flat was the people of my country. The experts sometimes describe the Congo Wars as Africa's World War. During this time some five million people were killed, most of them civilians.

What sort of land is Africa? It is a land full of many people of all colours, but mostly black people like me. It is a land of distances and a land of great variety. If you were to look down on Africa from space, you would see forests, grasslands, and deserts. And, as a continent, Africa is surrounded by beautiful oceans. There is also food everywhere, growing naturally. It has beautiful animals and birds. I am now an Australian citizen, but for me Africa will always be where I come from. For me, Africa will always be a paradise.

The country where I was born is the Democratic Republic of Congo, sometimes called Congo-Kinshasa, after Kinshasa, the capital city of the country. My home was in the lush highlands of Kivu, in the east of the Congo. My country is rich in resources, such as gold, minerals and coltan, an important component in computers and mobile phones, and rich in agriculture. And my country is also a country of great beauty, with forests, rich highlands and many rivers. The best known river is the Congo River, one of the largest in the world, but there are many rivers throughout the country, many of which run into the Congo River.

The Congo is a beautiful country, but a country which has been tortured through ruthless dictatorship, ethnic violence and war. I have suffered violent assault which has left me with permanent injuries, and have witnessed violent events. There is scar tissue of physical wounds, but there is also scar tissue of the heart. After many years of attempting to find refuge, I have at long last found a new home in Australia. I am proud to be an Australian citizen. I am, however, also proud of my Congolese heritage, and always will be. I am a survivor.

I grieve for my friends killed senselessly in the Congo Wars. I grieve for the victims of a ruthless dictator. I grieve for my friends and family killed in the ethnic violence in the Congo, most often brutally and without mercy. I grieve for my parents and brothers, killed in ethnic violence. But most of all I grieve for the loss of my home in Africa.

Small Change

Fiona Faulds

My mother carries her wallet like a child now. In it is little cash, maybe a couple of cards, where before it would be busting open with all sorts of things. Vagaries of her life spilling out if she picked it up the wrong way or, even worse, dropped it.

Like a child's purse, my mother's is flat and nearly empty, holding only a Library card and maybe a couple of coins with a button, unexpectedly and thrillingly found in odd places. Pulling it out to use, perhaps to capture some of that worthwhile value of her previous harried life, there is never any money in it, and she is reminded of her status. Laughing, also like a child, she brushes the exasperation of her diminished self aside (she must know we will pay) with a giggle or dismissive remark. At least a child doesn't remember anything different.

My mother has diminished in many other ways, not just those measured by the contents of her wallet. Her opinions seem forced, and her smile often brittle and tight. Once so busy doing it all, holding us all together, she rarely had time for a hug, let alone a cuddle. Now she is like the play-acting, wallet-grasping child; always reaching out for hugs, longing for a cuddle. We whip past her . . . awkward, not sure how to fall into a mothering embrace that is so foreign to us.

My mother was a serious hipster. She had a fabulous black faux fur jacket. She would go out at night in it looking beautiful, gleaming. Rushing out the door, always in a hurry, she would return later for me to bury my face into her, inhaling the exotic scents amongst her immense fur. I could lose myself in it, so relieved she had returned; as I knew she would, yet still relieved. Years later I realised the exotic smell was cigarette smoke, a smell that still takes me back to that thumping relief of her return.

She just did it all. Then before we knew it, she didn't anymore.

I wonder when our wallets and handbags and purses become something no longer needed. When we don't search for them anymore, as we go out to meet the world. When they become again the wallets of our childhood, reaching into them to find little there. Perhaps only a Library card, to borrow a book, which we have already read.

She Would

Lonnie Gilroy

She would round us up and march us out the front. She would make us sit in our chairs and watch her sunbathe on the grass. She would show us her belly and compel us to adore her and tell her how beautiful she is. She would show us her bowl and remind us it wasn't full. She would nudge our hands as we poured out biscuits, just to make sure we were giving her enough. She would tell us when it was her bedtime and make sure we followed her down the hallway. She would have a bath at the end of the bed and then snuggle up under the covers all night. She would wake us up in the middle of the night for a midnight snack, or to go to the bathroom, or for no reason at all—just for a walk around the house. She would be terribly rude to Dad. She would not care for visitors. She would love only Mum and me, and like a few other people, and barely tolerate the rest. She would cry a broken stuttering screech as if she lost her voice, though I think she was just putting it on for effect. She would bring us dead bugs as tribute. She would be the softest thing ever, apart from her claws which she would use if we weren't doing as we were told. She would love scratches around her cheeks and head and down her back. She would tempt you to rub her belly but punish you if you did. She would not just be part of the family; she would be in charge of the family. She would be the focus of every conversation. She would be our life.

This is what would happen if Kitty was still alive.

The Last Message

Mohammadreza Amiri

You never imagined living on a ventilator. When I put you in the car, you could still breathe and talk. 'Do we really need to go?' you said. 'Don't be a child dad!' I said. 'It's my age son, nothing else.' you said. You started showing the signs since last week. Your weak voice, pale face, shaking hands, wheezing sound, and dry coughs left no doubt that something was going on. 'I hate the Prince of Wales,' you said with your trembling voice. You meant the hospital.

You laughed at the doctor when he took a little blood sample from you. 'They just want to keep elderly men in the bed!' you said. 'Don't worry dad! Will stay with you tonight!' I said. You looked convinced. Then you asked for your phone, wanted to check your messages. 'Rachael is amazing in that blue dress!' you said. 'She will bring it with her' I said. 'Oh! Didn't know she is coming,' you said. A deep silence filled the room. You stared at me, expecting me to explain. 'Yes, she is coming for a wedding,' I said, but that was not the whole truth. 'It's great . . . just great . . .' you said. Your eyes became watery and your severe coughs started.

You gathered news from all TV channels that afternoon. I read a book on my phone. 'You're addicted to that thing!' you said. 'Just reading a book dad! That's all!' I said. 'I bet it is!' you said. Then turned off the TV and bent to put the remote on the side table. You dropped it. And then the coughs started once again. 'When will she be here?' you asked. 'At the airport now!' I said. You looked more curious. 'Well, Sydney or over there in Copenhagen?' you said. I smiled and said, 'No, not in Sydney!' You nodded and smiled. Darkness came in from the window. You slept and I continued reading.

An hour later, two nurses in masks and isolation gowns entered the room and took me with themselves. You did not even wake up. And I preferred that way. You remained on your own, so did I in a temporary quarantine. You were right about the doctor, he wanted to keep you for a while. They asked me if you lived with me. I told them I lived with you.

You texted me in the morning, holding on to your great sense of humour! 'There must be no disease that I haven't caught!' you said. You did not seem worried, tried to keep me calm instead. Your doctor informed me of your deteriorating situation. You would not like me to hear that. You were taken to the ICU in the afternoon. Your doctor cautiously told me, but he assured me everything was under control. You had a rough night, like many nights in your life, and finally surrendered at dawn, before Rachael landed. Your last message was: 'I love to see her in that blue dress!'

Screen of Death

Anna Chandler

It's eight days since GG died. Eight weeks since I saw her and sobbed on the flight from my childhood town back to Sydney. Days later, a national lockdown begins.

A crisp, lace tablecloth and a Lady Carlyle tea set now cover our usually bare wooden table. A plate of lamingtons waits next to our laptop. An internet address, the only directions we need to GG's funeral.

Connecting to the livestream, I can see on top of a coffin a framed, faded photo of a young, unfamiliar woman from another time. I know the body inside the casket has to be my 97-year-old grandmother because the woman in the front row of the funeral home is unmistakably my mother. I can also see seven relatives spaced 1.5 metres apart, unable to hold my mother's hand.

My husband comes into the kitchen, dressed in a suit, no shoes or socks. Freshly shaved. I wipe my tears with a lace hankie GG gave me years ago. Our two young daughters have tamed their hair and wear party dresses GG would have liked.

Our eldest confides as I light a candle, 'It's a bit like going to a wedding, isn't it Mummy?' My gut tightens as I say, 'Similar sense of occasion. Perhaps, not quite as much fun…'

A week earlier, I dialled into a meeting with the funeral director. 'Hear me, love?' she asks. It becomes clear she's had a crash course in technology when she explains the funeral will be 'streamlined'.

When the director and the photo slideshow (my responsibility) appear on our screen, the knot in my stomach loosens. Our mother is composed reading the eulogy. My sister's prerecorded piece begins smoothly, then, her face freezes for what feels like forever. The connection drops out. I text my sister. She's in another city watching the funeral, alone.

Me: Have you lost it entirely now? We have

Her: I'm just at the carnage that is me stage

Me: Farrk, I'm sorry

Her: It's not your fault

The dog barks. There's a thud at our front door. The groceries have been delivered. My sister's face remains stretched across the screen. Our kids suggest eating the lamingtons. GG wouldn't mind says the eldest.

The screen refreshes. We're back with our daughters singing a catchy hymn, recorded days earlier. The service finishes. *I Will Always Love You* plays. Our mother wails; my sister and I unable to console her.

The next day I email our relatives: 'Life isn't a dress rehearsal but apparently funerals have encores. Please see Grandma's edited memorial.' I like to think if GG—who loved a starring role in the Bowling Club recital—was looking down, she'd have approved. And scoffed; stupid, bloody computers.

Days later as our youngest is falling asleep, she whispers, 'was that GG in the box on the screen?' Since then, we've been navigating our children's first loss, the loss of GG and the loss of grieving together.

The Weight of His Breath

Anthony Lawrence

i.m. RHS

Tonight I'm remembering my friend who told me about the wild Banteng,
a breed of cattle in Arnhem Land, set free into the wild and, by extension,

the long history of feral introductions. When he spoke, with sadness,
about the filleting tables where he worked at the salmon farm, it was not

because of the chain-mail glove and knife, the entrails he'd heard could
clarify the future once you understood how to read them, or the blood

that pooled like archipelagoes on the floor, it was because of his deep,
unrequited love for a co-worker who wore her hair in plaits like fine

red rope, and whose scent, he swore, contained cedar shavings, moss,
and a rumour of vanilla. For years he skinned and vacuum-packed the fish,

kept his head down, and safeguarded hurt and nurture, in equal measure,
for the woman he coveted as friend and future lover. With his OCD's

involving all things black and white, he'd be driving and have to pull over
to retrieve a sheet of paper blown onto the road, or on the beach,

he'd fill his pockets with sun-bleached weed, driftwood, and bivalves
he'd prise from the rocks. Undiagnosed, yet on the spectrum, he'd sit

facing away from people at a dinner party, and eye contact was fleeting
and rare. He could take an outboard motor apart and reassemble it

as performance art, yet when it came to matters of the inner life,
the spark that lights the chambers of the heart, he'd falter, then drink.

In middle age, the singular life gave way to reclusiveness. He had
no phone, so you'd have to visit, his door closed, your knocks and calls

dying away. You'd wait and look for movement in the folds of a curtain,
for the sound of a man who knew how to hold the weight of his breath.

A master of tying knots, he could weave rope into beautiful designs,
giving each one a name, and he'd test them with the ute, driving off

with the rope fixed to a tree. No one knew he was close to his death,
and then news came through that he'd been found between a blackwood

branch and the ground. At his farewell, his fishing rod leaned against
the coffin. Now, when I hear gulls, I see him at the wheel of his boat,

talking quietly about the weather and the East Australian current,
as over his shoulder, an ocean monolith darkens and fades to black.

On his face, an expression that might be calm, or an early warning
sign of approaching storms.

Harbour

Sue Pincham

They met at the harbour the morning his father died. He was still carrying the green plastic bag from the hospital that held his father's belongings. They were few. He was tired and just wanted to sit and look at the boats and the water and they didn't say much.

When they said the lump in her breast was cancer, she cried, rang him and said, 'meet me at the harbour in half an hour.' They walked past the fishing boats and he cried when she told him and they walked along the cliffs and kept walking for miles. She did not know what else to do.

Soon there were all the medical things and operations and drugs and she was very tired most of the time. Her hair fell out and when she felt like eating again she suggested a picnic at the harbour. She had always enjoyed that. The cancer centre's psychologist had encouraged her to live in the moment and appreciate *now.* She tried to focus on the bobbing boats and the seagulls and the mouthfuls of food but it was no good. She didn't want to eat. She wanted to talk. And when she talked, she cried. And that was good. Her sadness was hers and she had a right to have it. The tears felt cleansing, healing.

When she died, he took her ashes to the harbour and scattered them near the lighthouse. It was what she wanted, what she had asked for.

'Do you think the seagulls might eat me?' she had asked. He didn't know if she was joking or not. He hadn't asked her. Now he wished he had.

He thought of all the times they had been here together walking for miles, or just sitting, talking or not talking.

Now he wasn't sure how he was going to put one foot in front of the other.

Ashes at Lake Monger

Amy Lin

for Trish

This blue container
seems to weigh more
as we get closer

because all that you were
is within these
plastic walls.

We're enclosed in domed blue,
by our own
atmospheric limit:
solid figures in a snowless globe,
the ones that don't dislodge
when shaken.

We pepper your ashes
between water reeds
and dry tree stumps -
where you played
make believe as a child,
imagined dead bodies
in the rushes.
Your ghoulish fantasies
are shards of shattered limits.
They still glint
in the wetlands' grasp.

Even your dust has a gradient.
Grey to white, so white.
Like sugar sieving into salt,
lining the beds with your sweetness.
Powdered smoke unfurls around us
and you fall   you float   you fly.

Billy

Peter Lach-Newinsky

Fall equinox, honey locusts starting their small-leafed rains
over the terrace, golden flecks
on Billy's black fur carried inside over tiles, blood-red carpet, tottering
his stiffening legs through his little pools of piss.

Digging his grave in the orchard near the bitter-tart cider apple,
the sun has broken through after a week of drought-breaking storm
and soft grey sheets of drizzle.   It's noon and a high eagle
circles in from the south,
one with the invisible water of its space.   This is where
the rabbits gather, a few rare earthworms
now gladden the desiccated heart like the tiny white puffballs
ballooning up from rain-dark soils,
or the full moon that night briefly unveiling its golden eye,
a bright hole among the wheeling clouds. The sun still
has some of its dog-days bite, the days of Billy's slow disassembling.

For weeks he has smelled increasingly of death, that sweet-rotten
nebula of incontinence and burnt onions. Always hungry
to feed his disappearing body, his last days meat-rejecting, his last
breakfast the maternal yoghurt I made.

Now seared in memory: the last time I see him shakily standing,
on the driveway   near the car, (beloved boot open, vet-ready),
looking up quizzically with confusion, trust, enquiry: 'Good. Are we
going on another great drive together?'   We lift him in.
As the tear tsunami tears in, my wife takes over the wheel.

He has shown us how to die as, for sixteen years, he has silently
shown us how to live, love,
his large soul, wide as Whitman, in the Now, unconditional,
unconditioned, his sheer joy of Being, including being sad,
fearful, angry, confused. A privilege to have known such a teacher.

Now grief grows its memory-loop tides as I talk to his many absences,
walking our wonted way together
around our twenty acres, he once ahead, then trailing, treat-goaded,
sniffing his creaking joints along our track, looking back
I wait for him, still, forever, as he crosses our dry creek.

The Phoenix

David McKenzie

I met The Phoenix when I was assigned as her social worker, after she lost her partner in the bushfires. He hid in his home-made bunker when the firestorm swept through his enclave, but it wasn't enough to save him. He was her secret partner. Not many people knew about them, so when he died the truth came out. She was exposed to the world, whether she wanted to be or not.

Sometimes she held tight to what he had bequeathed her; at other times, she pushed it all away. 'He's dead,' she would say. 'None of this really matters.' Yet it did matter, for it was all she had left of him.

I thought her strong. I told her she was strong. She thanked me with tears that flowed continuously. They flowed while she made tea, while she signed forms, and while she showed me his land which was now her land. It was like she had learned to live with the tears, to see through their shimmering veil. Her loss had indelibly changed her outlook.

She was rebuilding his house, but better. It would contain parts of him and parts of her. If their relationship had survived the fires, this is what it would have become. The government had a say too, with new building codes, but she managed to include all that without losing any of him. Her vision and creativity were remarkable.

Eighteen months later I said goodbye. She gave me a copy of *The Odyssey* as a parting gift. I treasure it still. And this was her message to me:

Now we come to the parting of our ways I'd like to thank you for all your care of me since we met. I am grateful for your gentle words, your strength and the 'silences'—when you just 'ignored' my private tears and gave me the time to 'get control' of the rest of my sentence. It made a very big difference to me to know that I had you ready to advocate for me if it all got too hard.

It's been a long and difficult journey. In the time we've had together I've learnt that you have a love of literature (a love that I also share). Therefore I decided to give you a book as a reminder of our time together. I could choose no better than Homer's 'Odyssey'—a classic tale of a long journey, many battles, and a fierce determination that eventually brought the weary traveller home. It's a story I hope to mirror.

Now it is over ten years later and I still think of her, of her grief. I believe her grief will be with her forever. The depth of her loss was immense; a hole that would take more than a lifetime to fill. I feel honoured she allowed me into her life when she was so vulnerable, her pain so exposed.

And I envy the love that leaves a grief so profound.

Gone

Jo Gardiner

Under a yellow moon
the house burned,
trees shed red,
shucked themselves black
in brittle showers.

Wind ruined the woodlands,
asked how you calculate
the half-life
of a twenty-year marriage;
how to know when the tipping point
meets the vanishing point;
how to tell when it's time
to master the art of disappointment,
to pay a debt of sorrow
and settle that old argument
between light and dark.

Giants

Gillian Barnett

We have come to an age of funerals.
Not my own. Not yet.
These are for the giants of our childhood,
uncles and aunts who loomed like laughing gods.
They married strong-minded equals,
refused to be called Uncle or Aunt,
said it made them feel old.
So, young they stayed, well into their eighties,
still talking loud, still driving fast.
It seemed age could not weary them.

Taught to stand tall, they did.
But the iron finger of age kept pushing,
slowly pushing into the back of their stiff necks.
One by one they learned to bow, just before the end.

I look at jumbled photographs as we empty my mother's home.
There they are, the tumultuous ten,
togged up for the nineteen-twenties, thirties and so on.
They brandish shotguns, men and women both.
(My parents met on a shooting trip.)
They dive from cliffs into rock pools,
light fires on remote beaches
—at least they were remote back then.
"We've had the best of it," my mother said.
She remembered when Brighton Cemetery was a mass of wildflowers
and stars shone bright above Melbourne.

There she is at Rye Back Beach with her sisters,
shrieking silently on old movie film as they
pull giant crayfish from pots lowered over the edge
and juggle them while standing on a treacherous reef.
Ocean depths suck at their feet
rehearsing for the seventh wave.

Now they've pulled themselves up as far as age allowed,
and marched off into the sunset
without a backward glance.

So we, who believed in them,
must endure a shrunken world.

for the unborn / this altered body

Olivia Hamilton

<table>
<tr><td>medicine
was made by men –
it could not conquer this</td><td>this excess
this disease
my body</td></tr>
<tr><td>what's the word for
losing
the unborn</td><td>missing, sacrificing
defeating, ending
pain</td></tr>
<tr><td>blue ocean blinding
I can almost see
their small brown forms
building sandcastles</td><td>inside this skin
the scalpel cut
an impossibility
from scarred flesh</td></tr>
<tr><td>there, see –</td><td>feel –</td></tr>
<tr><td>on that damp edge
between what is
and what never (now)
will be</td><td>a small incision
barely visible
adorns my skin
a brand</td></tr>
<tr><td>all is fine</td><td>how strange</td></tr>
<tr><td>all is fine</td><td>(I think)</td></tr>
<tr><td>all is fine</td><td>how strange it feels</td></tr>
</table>

what's the word for
learning
how to inhabit
this altered body

A Decision of Death

Naomi Gruneklee

I nod. The needle depresses and his breathing stops. It is done. Last night he had a strong heartbeat and now my credit card is maxed out on funeral costs. I am numb. I visit the local dog park and break the news to our friends. They are upset. Everyone says I made the right decision. This does not stop the guilt.

Stretch was an ex-working dog. At 11 years old he lost his owner, his balls, and half his teeth. I saw him online and visited the Lost Dogs Home. It was my lucky day. Before I knew it, I was driving home with a beautiful Kelpie for the bargain price of $50 with a bed and blanket included. We played fetch all afternoon.

Stretch quickly became a favourite at any park we visited. He loved fetch and many people ignored their own dogs to play with mine. He had no interest in other toys. Fetch was his life. And he was mine.

One day he started limping. Diagnosis cancer. Solution: amputate the leg. Could a three-legged dog play fetch? Yes. He recovered quickly and even played fetch with his best friend. But our happy life was not to last. A few weeks later Stretch deteriorated. He had cancer throughout his body. Solution: chemo drugs. He needed 24/7 care. I did everything from a mattress next to his bed—cried, worked, ate, slept. I used a sling to help him walk and carried him if we went too far. I booked a dog physio to help strengthen his muscles. Blood results indicated the chemo was working.

I had cabin fever and Stretch was sleeping. I went out. I returned an hour later and Stretch was frantic. He had spun himself on the blanket but could not get up. He yelped when I picked him up. I lay him on the grass outside whilst I returned for his sling. But my dog was never going to stand nor walk again. I needed help. The vet offered to send someone to euthanize Stretch. I refused the offer through my tears. I was not ready for that. Stretch and I lay on the grass in the sun.

Stretch was royalty. We carried him into the specialist's on a blanket-laden board. This was my last resort. I already knew the solution but needed professional confirmation. They said he had a strong heartbeat. He yelped when they tried to lift him and confirmed my suspicions. I wanted his last breaths to be at home so they gave him morphine for the pain.

It has been seven months since I played God. The dog food and most toys have been re-distributed but the delivery from the crematorium remains unopened. The blankets are being used to warm foster cats. I still relive Stretch trying to remove the needle used to stop his final breaths and a voice in my head questions if I did everything I could before making the decision.

I always liked that country

Amanda Jarasius

It is a slowing down

Breaths becoming sparser, the space between drawing in and exhalation expanded

Skin retreating further towards bone . . .

. . . it's only human for fourteen days without food to begin to show

After he woke up, despite his best efforts, because the laws here still don't allow for what he really wanted

There was emancipation in little doses dispensed by kindly nurses, bottled relief manufactured in India

That place where the dead are carried through Varanasi streets, wrapped in white, held together by ropes

and weighted down with stones

Hungry for liberation by the Ganga River

I always liked that country, he said through a hoarse trachea

His humour unlike his voice, didn't need aid

The same week my mother put the dog down

Was the same week the space between his drawing in and exhalation of breath became endless

We all knew it was coming

Still, I don't understand why my mother had to put the dog down that same week

I guess maybe a farewell was already in the air

Drifting like white through water in the Ganga

Nonna

Hannah Smith

A cold enough day. Not melancholic. The smell won't tear me.
Blue, gold, red. I'll flash in the sun. A gold coin on the pavement.
Thanks! It was Nonna's.
I know right! See. It's lined. See. The wool doesn't scratch. See. Shoulder pads!
Outlook. Inbox (1). Reply.
Musty. Hard to describe. Johnson & Johnson Talcum Powder. Slapped on wrinkling skin after a shower. Tuesday and Thursday afternoons of chips, lemonade, Arthur, CatDog. Pikelets in the dark Smith Family store. Shepherd's pie, boiled beans, triangles of buttered bread. The silverware for a special occasion. Jiggling jelly and cream trifle. The white cheeked heron. First bird you taught me. Binoculars. Thermos of tea. Shortbread. Folding chairs by the Toyota Camry. The Women's Weekly Children's Birthday Cake Book. This year a fairy please.
I won't wash it.
Then Slowly. In Time. Microwave dinners. A rail on the stairs. A nurse in the mornings. Portly to slight. Memory fades. How's Sydney? Still got that job? How are your flatmates? How's Sydney? Still got that job? How are your flatmates? How's Sydney? Still got that job? How are your flatmates?
I won't wash it.

I don't want to worry you. When's your next day off? You should come to Newcastle. I could be wrong. It could be weeks. It could be months.

I'll just finish this email. Then I'll come. Outlook. Inbox (1). Reply.

Pack. Train. She's just having a lay down. We'll heat up her dinner. She can have it in bed.

What a surprise.

Tray wobbles on her bony knees.

How's Sydney?

Swallows a mouthful.

Still got that job?

Winces.

How are your flatmates?

Good Nonna. Yes Nonna. Good Nonna.

I'm short with her. Almost rude. I don't want her to talk. She's wheezing.

I open the wardrobe. To distract her? To distract me? Look at all these wonderful clothes you have Nonna! Look at how hip you are Nonna! Look at this beautiful jacket. Blue, gold, red. I bet you'd flash in the sun Nonna. A coin glinting on the pavement Nonna.

At the Cancer Retreat

Kevin Smith

Outside our room the sun burns the grass
brown with rays brutal as a welder's
flame. Kangaroos lounge in frail shade
knowing more than most how to outwait
the heat; the bush bakes in an oven. Before
dawn we walked to a creek steeped in the leaves
of tea trees bowing their heads on its banks, and laid
in shallow water that gave us much but couldn't
wash away her illness.

A hot wind rises
and slowly dies among the gums and over
paddocks. Soon a bell will call us in
and we will shuffle among those losing their shoes
to journey barefoot toward a cure. The bush
crackles; it shrinks back into itself. And there,
the bell, the footfalls too, and the muffled talk
of those who've come to take their lives by the scruff
of their necks and hang the harder questions out
to dry. The sky's as luminous and blue as any
sea I'd like to sail away on, tacking
close to the wind for somewhere else. In the kitchen
garden chickens scratch the ground for worms.

I Can't Grieve the World This Year

Kate Olivieri

I can't grieve the world this year
When it didn't grieve for me
My things all gone in flood
Covered in muddy debris

I can't grieve the world this year
When I was left alone
Seven weeks of pregnancy
Empty belly, on my own

I can't grieve the world this year
Though it's hard not to be free
It's nice to stay at home
It's pretty good for me

I can't grieve the world this year
I'm busy, I'm sorry, I'm done
You'll have to grieve yourself
I'm looking after my little son

Guilt

Laura Fox

The hardest thing about grief is the guilt that comes with it. Society only allows us to grieve for certain things. There is always someone worse off than us. But does that make our grief less important? The thing is, according to others, I am selfish. Self-centred. Arrogant. Because I grieve for something that still exists. My life. Just a version of my life that is now over.

I am a mother. My baby changed my life in every conceivable way. But I am not allowed to grieve for the life I had, or the person I was, because I am lucky.

I am not allowed to be sad about the clothes that used to fit me, the sleep I used to have, or the sense of accomplishment I felt at being an active and contributing member of society. I should be quiet, stay at home and feel lucky.

I shouldn't grieve for the time my husband and I used to have—time to do anything, go anywhere, be frivolous, spend money, drink too much wine—because we are lucky.

I did not have an easy induction into motherhood. My baby was breech and she was born via caesarean section. It isn't the easy way out, as society wants you to believe. The drugs made me sick and I was in pain—but I couldn't complain, because I am lucky. My baby didn't sleep, she also didn't eat. She refused to breastfeed, she screamed. She didn't gain weight, and I was in a constant state of anxiety. Before she was born I had never suffered from anxiety. But I am not allowed to grieve for that person—that well rested, non-anxious person—because I am lucky.

There is no handbook. But there are rules. Dictated to new mums by everyone else. The unsolicited advice; a sense of how we should feel; the overwhelming love for our babies that is supposed to be instant; the act of having it all together. And as a result we are treading water, pasting on smiles, trying not to fall in a heap and certainly not allowed to grieve for the people we were.

Do I know that I am lucky? Absolutely. But I am still human. My feelings may not be expressed often, socially accepted, or as important as yours, but they are mine, and they are valid.

I am no longer just a woman, a wife, a teacher, a daughter, a sister, a friend, or someone who had the privilege of sleeping all night—and let me tell you, I took that privilege for granted for many many years. I am now a mother. And it has taken me seven months to grieve for the person I was, accept the person I am, and try every day to reconcile the two.

James Dean's Brother

Colin Young

I think of you as the clouds
outside my lounge window
drift and reform their tendrils
or dissolve into blue.
I'd only known you a short while,
slept with you, smelt your fragrance,
before you took your own life.

At one time you were everything
to me. We held each other so tight
I could hear your breath.
You told me little about your past
or family. But as for James Dean,
whose posters were strewn over
your bedroom walls, I felt
he was your long-lost brother.

You said he died at twenty-four,
a year you were approaching,
like a freight-train to a crossing.
I asked about your parents,
but you were unmoored from them
long ago. Your face looked away
into the distance then.

How I remember our lips
meeting fused, and the heat
of your desperation. We lay
often wrapped up in silence.
No words now for your absence.
Rustle of leaves reminds me
only of you. The frail
branches flex to the breeze.

dad

Colin Campbell

he is digging   treading the manure
into the earth and then covering it
again and again until it is done
and he and the years between them
have turned the yellow clay into a garden
and the robin is happy and sings about it
and the thrush thrashes a snail

he is busy in his greenhouse
where the tomatoes cluster like grapes
rich and glossy   his hands are green with juice
and hold that smell of rich growth and duty
and he waters most evenings   quietly

he is cleaning the windows   grinning through
the glass   his cap tipped back   scraping
the suds from the panes   polishing   busy
' 'cause Mum can't do it no more, can she?'

and now he's gone   and so's his garden
his rickety green-house and his fruit
he could lay a hedge   plough a field
single beet   build a stack   milk a herd
and do countless other things skills that have gone with him
for they are no longer needed
he used to say, "a machine can do it all today
they don't need blokes like me no more"

there are no poppies in the corn now or docks or thistles
and the landscape is still and empty of other things too
like elms and lapwings
and this solitary skilful man—he who toiled under a wide Suffolk sky
in a green and growing world—
is now a fading figure with the sun behind him
and his stretched shadow momentarily
lay across the paths that we have travelled
and we rested   and he fed us
in the shade he made for us.

Mostly It Comes In Waves

Una Hurding

Mostly it comes in waves.
But always that background trickle of water
Like continual tinnitus.
Mostly it comes in waves.
Suddenly out of the depths
While emptying the bins,
Walking the dog,
Annoyingly, midsentence with friends.
Then throughout the spasmodic, sleepless night.
If you look for it, give it attention,
It's a smash and grab operation
Sweeping you up and dragging you out to sea.
Unbidden, the tsunami hits hardest;
Sucking the breath from you,
Holding you under,
Pummelling, sadistic, merciless.
But just sometimes it's that delicate music
From the seashell I hold to my ear.

Kiddo, Confused

Celeste McDermott Healey

Flo's car swings into the station's carpark at four-thirty exactly. She toots the horn as she pulls up next to where I am sitting on the curb. Flo leans out through the open window with one arm across the back of the passenger seat headrest.

Hiya, kiddo. Hop in.

You're late, I say, and stand as she pops the car's boot. I place my backpack in and slam it shut.

Four-thirty, she says, but it's a little uncertain, almost a question. I pull open the passenger door with a little more force than necessary. I still haven't met her eyes. I feel tired and grimy from the train trip and irritable at being called kiddo.

Three-thirty, I say. You obviously just didn't double check.

We pull out of the station and onto the highway. I turn my head to look out the window as the trail of houses goes from cottages to farms, and then into the rolling green hills of the countryside. It has been raining, of course, and a light mist has settled like a soft mosquito net over the fields. The air is hot and heavy and I can taste the fresh saltiness of the evening thunderstorm to come.

I'm sorry, Flo says, but it's a few beats too late, like she's been thinking how best to phrase something that she's not even sure she should be saying. I also know that she is apologising for something that she doesn't need to apologise for but I can't bring myself to say anything in return. We sit in silence for a few beats.

Flo sighs and flicks the indicator to turn left into our street. Are you okay? she says as we pull up to the house. My mother's house.

I puff my cheeks and blow the air out quickly and say, I don't know, Flo. What do you think?

Me?

We're about to bury our mother who hated me from the moment she gave birth to me. I'm not okay, but I'm also not not okay. I wait another beat and then say, I'm just very confused.

Flo parks the car and turns to me in her seat. She presses her lips together and swipes gracefully at a piece of my hair that has fallen out from behind my ear. The gesture is so precise, so particular in its familiarity, that I see my mother behind the blue of her eyes, just for a flash.

She loved you, you know.

Peculiar way of showing it, I say, and reach for the door handle.

Flo touches my knee with her hand to stop me, just lightly, and leans forward to place a kiss on my forehead. I get out of the car in silence and pull my backpack from the boot and head towards the front door.

Dinner with Da is at eight o'clock, Flo calls out to my back.

I wave in recognition but also in dismissal. I won't be there.

Adults Can't Be Orphans

Sherry Mackay

'The hospital rang; your mum died in the night.' My father had woken me up just after sunrise. It was mostly dark outside with a hint of red and gold breaking out to the east. I got out of bed, made us tea and toast, then put on my clothes and headed to work. It was Saturday morning, and I was rostered on at the library. I drove on auto-pilot, parked, went into the library, said good morning to my assistant. We didn't talk much. After a couple of hours, I turned to her and said: 'I don't really feel like being here today.'

'Me neither.' She shrugged, turned back to the books, and kept putting them on the shelves.

'My mum died this morning.' She looked at me like I was a swamp creature, her confusion at my presence showing on her face. I barely understood why I had come in to work but I knew I had to pretend for a little longer that everything was the same. 'As long as I keep on doing the same things that I was doing before dad woke me, my life will go on being the same. I can make it all go away, if I just keep on shelving books, and answering queries, and pretending that nothing earth-shattering and terrifying has happened at all.'

For a little longer, I can push grief away, that greedy beast that grips me by the arms, and hangs on, grasping me tighter and tighter until I can barely breathe, until I'm left an exhausted, empty husk. I may look the same but I am no longer that woman, that daughter with a mother. Shake me and you can hear the grief rattle around my bones.

A few years later, an interstate phone call. My stepmother, telling me that my father was dead. She was a drug addict and a drunk who had enticed my disabled dad into a fog of booze and drugs. She said that he'd died in her arms, with a sigh and a last, loving look into her eyes. I knew this was a fairy story, a tale woven to make me feel better. 'Did she even bother to call an ambulance?' I wondered.

There was a funeral, and tears, and her plea to remain in touch. I refused. How could she ask me? This befuddled woman, barely older than me, who had swept into our lives, and swept out again, carrying off the family possessions and my dad's life. The police rang to tell me there had to be an autopsy because it was a sudden death. Dad was dead at the age of just fifty-five. A heart attack, they said.

So now I am an orphan. The dictionary declares you're not an orphan if you're over eighteen. But I am still a daughter; motherless, fatherless but a daughter. The parents who made me have left this world, and I am indeed an orphan.

Birthing A Memory

Nicole Moore

After the birth of my daughter, I began having nightmares. Every single night I would go to sleep and find myself sitting as a nine year old in a primary school classroom. I would sit there, waiting impatiently, blatantly aware that at any given moment, the deputy principal would arrive with the news of my father's death and I would wake, confused and terrified.

Some nights it would only take minutes to reorientate myself, others I would lie awake for hours watching the clock slowly tick over and questioning why my mind had chosen now to begin to relive one of the worst days of my life. After a while, however, I found the answer.

One of the worst elements of grief suffered as a child is the dread that it creates in your mind as you contemplate whether history may be cruel enough to repeat itself. It does not matter how many therapists you talk to, how many hours you spend delving into your inner psyche or how ridiculous you understand those thoughts to be, they linger and burrow into your soul. *What if*, they question? Because, after all, you know that it can happen. You understand that a parent can be forced to leave their child.

So, when you go to bed, you strive to keep your eyes open and fixed on a black and white static screen so that you don't lose sight of your sleeping baby. You strain your ears to hear any sound, because you know that bad things happen to good people, and you revert to the scared child trying to comprehend the unfathomable loss of a parent.

You make promises to your own child that you pray you can keep. Promises that you will always be there and that you will be able to provide. Yet, you also write farewell letters, just in case, because you know what it feels like to not be granted that closure.

You begin to grieve a loss that has not yet occurred, a loss of self, a loss of confidence and strength and you begin to become a different person, altered by grief and by fear. Yet, in an odd way, you also become stronger and more defiant, daring death to a duel because no one, you argue, could be more determined to win.

Eventually, you find a way to sleep at night by focusing not on what was lost but what was gained. You focus on the independence and strength that you found as a child being forced to become an adult. You learn to accept the uncertainty.

And each night before you go to bed, you carry your child outside and say Good night to Pa Star and acknowledge that history belongs in the past.

Ave atque vale

Denise O'Hagan

The wind was getting up as we set out
Plastic bags ballooned down High St
Snaring lamp-posts, mobbing gutters
As the rain began to fall.

Death shrinks us like a doll
And in the steely presence of it
You feel gauche and graceless,
To even be alive.

It was her and it was not her
Casketed in black and lace
Stilled and scarfed and lipsticked
Fingers threaded through with beads.

In the unsteady candlelight
I thought of many things
The glint of hairpins in the kitchen
And painted Easter eggs.

How she didn't mind if I skipped school
As long as I did my Latin,
And statues draped on sarcophagi
In marbled symmetry.

But she was no saint, my mother
She liked her drop of red, swore behind the wheel,
Spurned coffee mornings to read and write
And didn't attend Tupperware parties.

She'd been made up, of course.
But the parchment line between skin and bone
Was tangible, tufts of eyebrow barely visible
And her pale rounds of eyelids shone like bone.

The still vein on the underside of her wrist
Gave it all away. And the skirt I'd pressed on her,
Softly stretchy and unfashionably forgiving
So she could dress without bending so much.

Because that whole last year
She was already
Half-way
Here.

Note: 'Ave atque vale' were the words written by the Roman poet Catullus to commemorate his brother. Loosely translated, they mean 'Hail and farewell'.

Loss

Abby Donkin

Today is the first day she stopped crying. Her face is worn: her eyes so swollen that the skin of her upper and lower lids fold into multiple red rolls and her cheeks draw downward. Three days. She's hardly eaten anything. I don't remember seeing her cry like this before. In her twenties now, although it shouldn't make a difference, it does to her.

Across the table, past the vase with flowers showing early signs of death, she sits there with her head tilted downward. She's not paying attention to the conversation at the table, but neither am I. She catches me staring and lazily offers me a smile. My attention is derailed when I hear my name.

'Joe,' my Dad says, 'Pass me the potato and gravy, mate.' I pass the takeaway tub filled with white and brown ooze. Is it even gravy?

Neither Mum or Dad have cooked since last Friday, unless you count toasted sandwiches as cooking. They both have a weird way of coping with loss. Mum doesn't speak his name but keeps herself busy with crosswords, and Dad just does weeding in the garden when he is home. And me. Well, I don't know how to feel or if I need to do anything different. Sad, sure, but I'm just going about my regular business.

My sister, she's devastated. It's unlike her though, she's usually the rational one: the cool cucumber when shit hits the fan. She holds her cards close to her chest when it comes to her own emotions, the supportive one when someone else is going through crap.

Openly vulnerable now, grieving the loss of her eight-year-old dog, her best mate, Shep. She loved that dog. Strange to me, but she really confided in that dog. I came home early one afternoon from uni and heard her talking. She didn't realise I'd come through the backyard gate, because Dad had a bout of Mr. Fixeritus the weekend before and tightened all the gate's wrought-iron hinges and latch.

She stood at the washing line with her back to me, pegging her clothes to dry. The giant German Shepherd laid at her feet, he raised his head as if to say he knew I was there, but he didn't stir. My sister hadn't noticed; she continued talking to the dog. 'I feel alone in this world, buddy.' She finished pegging her jeans and crouched down to face Shep. 'I cannot tell anyone, but you. I don't want my parents or anyone to worry, y'know? And I'm a little embarrassed.' She pats the scruff of Shep's full neck. 'But at least I've got you mate.' That struck me to hear her say these things. She always had it together, kind, helpful, had many friends around her. But I never knew she was lonely, and now she is more than ever.

That's what I need to do - let her know I am here for her. She hasn't lost me.

Shadow

Russ Talbot

Grief stalks me like a sniper
Holding me in its sights
Waiting for a clean shot.

More Than a Thousand Pieces

Gillian Telford

The older children are absorbed in their Christmas jig-saw;
quick minds, deft fingers; sorting, fiddling, often pausing
to study the picture-lid. Now and then I hear, 'Yay, got it!'

With the youngest, I share a wooden form board; we're making
people, finding body parts to fit into place, heads, trunks, arms,
legs — little fingers twiddling pegs, 'look Granny, it's a lady.'

I'm there, but not there — part of me watching over the children
while seeing for the first time, how my own puzzle has begun
to disassemble. All those pieces — gathered, fitted together

over years of shared moments. Like pictures on lids, every
box containing parts of my life — but those in the pictures, who
knew me well, who knew how it *really* was, those friends, one

by one, are disappearing. And as they go, they take not only
themselves, they take their insight of all we shared —
how we laughed in staff-meetings, helped pack up homes,

wept over children, spilt raspberry jam. Now, only I know
who I was back then— hear wind in the power-lines, watch
from a window. Are we ever more than a random collection?

'Look,' says the little one, 'now I'm taking out all the pieces.'

Grieve, Breathe, Grieve

Thy Pham

My mother has miscarried.

It's unspoken. The baby bump is less prominent. Her appetite seems to have whittled down; her smiles have become a valuable currency—I would trade my existence for a single one. Replacing them is a thin, firm line and downcast eyes. The catalogue for baby clothes lies untouched, tossed onto the kitchen bench. She barely speaks, and when she does, it's something mundane like 'breakfast' or 'dinner.'

We no longer talk about the puffiness around her eyes, or the remaining bump on her belly, a painful reminder of failure. Our car rides are filled with pop music and radio show blabber. It's convenient; it drowns out the silence.

I pretend not to notice the increased frequency of closed doors. Through the cracks of her bedroom door I often see a figure placing a gentle arm over her. Sometimes it is my father, sometimes it is my aunt. I always hear the wracking sobs and the quiet, mourning howl that emerges. I always stay on the sofa. What's there to say?

I learn to stop placing my hand on her belly. I learn not to ask. This has been confined to a space reserved for bitter memories.

As I am older, it is only now that I realise. The pain to have had a life within you, growing with you, torn away at the last minute. To go from feeling the faint kicks to nothingness. To wake up every day and look at the nursery, the clothes and tiny socks, knowing that it will only be covered by dust. To see the ultrasounds and no child.

So, I cry. I cry for her and for others who have lost. I allow myself to weep for them, for my sibling, for myself.

Grieve. Breathe. Grieve.

In this moment, I commemorate the grief we all have. It may not always be visible. Sometimes it is a kite, anchored lightly to our shoulders. Sometimes it is tightly latched onto our backs, engulfing us such that we cannot fling it aside. We learn to acknowledge its existence and allow it to grow with us as we experience other griefs. Loss—of a career, a friendship, a relationship, a person. Death—of a loved one. And with this, denial, anger, guilt, mourning, coping and finally, acceptance.

We are constantly deconstructed then reconstructed.

I only pray that we will heal.

A Lock of Hair

Judy Dally

After the funeral
they gave me
this lock of your hair

tied with purple ribbon
and tucked into
a little cardboard box.

Your surname
is written on the box
in black ink.

The lock of hair
is soft to the touch
and curled in a perfect circle.

Your hair
was always thick
and unruly

unlike mine: thin and fine;
always fair and now
unnaturally blonde.

Unlike our mother's;
mousey brown
and now white as snow.

Unlike our father's:
flat and black
with a Hitlerish slick.

I don't know what to do
with this lock of your hair.
Perhaps it should be

preserved in resin
or kept in a golden locket
but it lies coiled

in its cardboard coffin
like a spring.
I need to take it

to some beautiful windy place;
hold it gently
between my fingers

then
let you go.

Goodbye, My Daughter

Diana Smith

Up until a year ago, I thought I was familiar with all types of grief. The grief that comes with migration, then a divorce. The devastation of my father's death. All different types of sorrow. All different ways of saying goodbye.

I walked in on my teen daughter on the phone changing an appointment time with someone. I asked her who she was seeing, worried she was sick, and she replied that it was a counsellor.

'Why?'

She looked at her girlfriend and said, 'So, how do I tell my mother?'

'Tell me what?' I asked, completely perplexed.

'Mum, I have to have counselling because I want to transition into a boy. I feel like I am in the wrong body. I feel like on the inside, I'm a male, and I want to look like one too.'

How could she and I be so close and I not see this? We had always talked about everything . . . or so I thought! With my head spinning I wondered, how do I process this?

I did not know it was something people even did! I looked at photos of her growing up and she is so beautiful. How could she not be happy looking in the mirror? I felt complete shock, feeling sick in the pit of my stomach. I just wanted to protect her. I knew this would be tough and that people wouldn't understand. Hell, I could barely understand it and I was her mother! I was brought up with the statement, 'God doesn't make junk.' I just couldn't fathom how you could be so unhappy being you.

I did what any self-respecting clueless mum would do; I researched. On YouTube there were so many stories of people transitioning, from male to female and female to male. I tried hard to understand their point of view. We went to counselling together and eventually I realised that no matter what gender she became, she would always be my child, and my baby. I would still love her with all my heart. So, I came to accept the decision and support her in this journey. At the end of the day a glass of wine helped!

I have days I just cry, missing the girl she used to be. She was always a tomboy but this was about changing her entire body. And, as she is over 18, it's ultimately her choice. Luckily, she understands our struggle to change our words from *she* to *he* after all these years. After wearing a binder for two years, and hating her chest with a passion, she finally had top surgery last month. Although it was a painful process, she is so much happier. You see it in her posture, the way she walks; she is so much more confident.

Saying *she* just seems wrong now. We will get there eventually. Although I am so sad at losing my beautiful daughter, my arms and heart are open, welcoming the arrival of my son.

Strange

Elizabeth Macintosh

Strange.

My mother achieved her goal of dying at home but not in the way that she would have wanted.

On a hot January afternoon, Mum was found on the timber ramp at the front of her house, her body pointing towards the door, shoeless. Despite the fact that in her 88 years, she always wore shoes. Strange. Her wheelie walker was on the wooden veranda, beyond reach. Despite the fact that she consistently sought its security after falling heavily in a car park and breaking her hip. Strange. Her sensible dark shoes were found, in reverse position, underneath a green plastic chair. Despite the fact that she never sat there. Strange.

Mum had fallen face first, her nose smashed in, arms by her side. There was no indication that she had tried to save herself. It was as if she had been standing there, someone tapped her on the shoulder and she'd toppled over. Strange.

The paramedics called the police who decided it was a crime scene. Despite the fact there was no evidence of robbery, her purse was intact and nothing in the house disturbed. Strange.

My sister arrived. Anne wasn't allowed to pat Mum's hair, hold her hand or say goodbye in the way she wanted. She identified the body.

'It was her but it wasn't her,' recounted Anne, over and over. 'You could tell it was her but it wasn't her.'

My mother was zipped into a body bag and loaded into a hearse as my sister watched. Peak hour traffic crawled by. There was no privacy or dignity in death. Mum was a very private lady who would have been horrified if she'd had an inkling of what would transpire after her death at home.

Sleepless, Anne sat all night on her own back veranda, staring at the speckled sky and drinking copious amounts of tea. Over 500 kilometres away, I swallowed a sleeping pill.

The funeral couldn't be planned until the coroner determined whether an autopsy was necessary. In holiday season, the backlog of cases meant it could be months before the body was released to a funeral home. Already grieving Mum's death, the uncertainty made it more distressing.

When the coroner decided an autopsy unnecessary, Anne wanted to view the body. Everyone advised against it, the morticians vehement.

Anne was distraught. 'But I didn't get to say goodbye. I couldn't touch her. It was a crime scene.' There was no closure for her.

On the day of the funeral, she sat convulsing beside me in the front row of the chapel, the cedar coffin only two metres away.

Weeks later, Anne bushwalked alone in the bleak light of dawn. She came upon a healthy female koala sitting in the middle of the dirt track, unmoving, placid. Anne crept up beside it. The koala returned her gaze. Strange. Anne moved past and when she returned, it was gone. Was this a sign that Mum had passed over? We would like to think so.

Father's Day

Fiona Lynch

She boards the 'Bathurst bullet' at Springwood
station, twenty-something juggling backpack,
books, careful not to crush the long stems.
She unpacks, settles in, checks her phone,
smiles. I admire them. *They're my Dad's—*
he loves growing orchids.

Past the window—your purple-throated rhodies,
feathery cosmos in terracotta, tomatoes split
with pride, battles lost to cabbage moth.
And raspberries, warm from the picking—
long before fresh manure made them a killing
field—third-degree burns, a Calvary of trussed

corpses. Remember the green gage plum behind
the back gate? Victim to unbridled pruning.
You, a ladder and a handsaw—a low-budget
circus. In the interests of anything green, I said
there should be a secateur registration authority.
You wouldn't have made probation Dad.

God save the roses I miss you. Laughing
at yourself, at the bodies buried in the garden,
nothing ever beyond redemption, as compost.
A thousand cuts—missing orchids you never
grew—and probably would have murdered.

The dying season

Andrew Taylor

vale Ian Taylor

Summer is the dying season –
trees on the cliff opposite have lost
their leaves, grass in the park
has retreated underground, the air
breathes smoke from the bushfires
strangling towns, razing farms
and suffocating the city. Our clothes
and I'm sure our hair smell of ash.
And in a distant town almost
choking with memories a long life
has breathed out and is gone.
There was no drama, no defiant
resistance, nothing but the quiet end
of a life lived fully and finally
dwindled to a point. Beyond that
only some grief, and the careful ebb
of the river that he loved and the slow
return – as it always does – of the tide.

27.12.2019

Mr Bruce

Amelia Gibson

Mr Bruce was my English teacher. He was a gruff man that refused to take any crap from students and was matter of fact with his feedback, which some perceived as harsh. He wasn't a favourite of many. I appreciated his honesty and being treated as an adult capable of handling the truth, rather than needing to be shielded from it.

None of us thought much of it when he went home sick. We were left to our own devices; the more industrious went straight to homework, while the less motivated retrieved their mobile phones or chatted idly.

The following day, the atmosphere was an odd mixture of sombreness and commotion. I immediately knew something was wrong. I was shocked when a friend told me that Mr Bruce had died of a heart attack.

I would never forget the look on Miss Carmody's face when she spoke to us during our third period English class. She was a butch, grey-haired woman with a pixie cut, renowned for being tough.

Today she didn't look tough at all; she was red-faced with grief. A tear shed from her eye when she informed us that when Mr Bruce left, he said, 'I feel so ill I could cark it.' Her voice almost broke getting the words out. An uncomfortable lump formed in my throat at her visible anguish and refused to be swallowed down. One of my classmates, a popular, kind-hearted blonde girl, was in tears.

Miss Carmody advised us that the English faculty would be taking the afternoon off. We could stay here together or join our classmates in the playground. We all sat in silence for a full ten minutes in a show of solidarity; a mark of respect. I felt tears prickle at the corner of my eyes as they lingered on Mr Bruce's empty desk.

After a few minutes, the grave atmosphere weighed too heavily on us. My classmates started to leave, some alone, some with an arm around each other. We all had our own way of dealing with it.

Our class were permitted to go to his funeral. Some of us chose not to. I wanted to pay my respects.

We stood at the back of the room. At the front were his family: his wife, a pretty dark-haired woman. His children; a teenage boy and girl, and a young boy of primary school age. He looked so small. That painful lump resurfaced at the thought. I tried to swallow it down.

My eyes travelled at last to Mr Bruce's coffin, his photograph propped on top. *He's in there*, the thought hit me. This obvious thought triggered a pang akin to panic, followed by a great wave of distress. I tried not to cry. I wanted to be strong. But then I remembered a play we studied with him:

'To weep is to make less the depth of grief.'- William Shakespeare, King Henry VI

I no longer tried to hold in the tears.

The Day You Died

Julia Kaylock

Our lives touched briefly, and ended unsatisfactorily—for me, anyway. I never called you 'Mother'. Did you think of me as 'your child'? Did you ever see my face, sense my lust for life, feel my newborn skin, breathe my baby scent? I don't know, I can't ask you. Neither can I ask you what it was like, giving birth and giving me away. I can't ask if you grieved my loss, although I believe you did, if only because you saw the need to tell your husband (not my father) about me on your deathbed.

I was twenty-seven when I discovered I was adopted, eleven years or so after the date of your death. As pieces of the puzzle started working themselves into the new narrative of my life, I mourned the old life I had led and taken as truth. The people I called family were not my flesh and blood. This, I could have forgiven, but not the lies that only served to create a wedge between myself and my adoptive parents, who gradually retreated from our relationship. Once the child whose arrival helped to distance them from the grief of infertility, I had reminded them of it all over again. Relatives blamed me for a lack of consideration, gratitude, respect. No-one acknowledged my shock, anger and disbelief. For a long time afterwards, I tried hard to still show love, trying to assuage their grief, denying my own.

Finally, at age thirty-three, extreme grief appeared in a flash, shattering my world. As I looked at my own two young daughters, your grandchildren, and realised they had no real heritage to draw on, I knew I had to find you. Amazingly, after all the waiting time, the true story materialised on a single day; I found you, and lost you in the space of a heartbeat. I discovered you had died when I was sixteen, an outcome I had not imagined. The social worker at the hospital who gave me your surname—*my* surname—was kind, but distant. The young cousin who had unwittingly encumbered me with the heartbreaking news had no concept of my despair; he suggested I call his brother, who had been compiling the family tree. For me, this was the day you died.

The old me was gone and now I'd never know myself through your eyes. I found myself grieving your death, the mother I never knew. Thus began a lifetime of grief; despite feeling a strong bond with our relatives, who welcomed and accepted me, I was without a sense of kinship. Counselling taught me about separation-anxiety, a kind of PTSD-induced trauma that can lead to a sense of unbelonging and alienation. Like many adoptees, I have a chronic fear of abandonment that once identified, I began to take steps to overcome. I will always feel alone, but cherish the glimpses of you through stories, photos and mementos; these help to lessen the persistent pain of grief.

Still

Sophia Moore

In the corner of some dark, dingy bar
In the window of some dark, dingy bar
There is a reflection of us
We are still wearing jeans
And heavy coats

corner table

Linda Brooks

Winter's blast enters with me
slamming the glass door to the café.
You're already here, pretending
not to wait, holding your gaunt frame erect

You move when you see me, stepping
forward with careful pace, waving
a pale tight-skinned hand, choosing
the table in a sunlit corner.

You've aged twenty years in two, so thin
you almost fold in half. Wanting
news on the cancer, I lean in to hope.
'I didn't get the email attachment,' I say.

The left corner of your mouth jerks
the way it always has. You release
a deep sigh, then details: biopsies
late stages, medications, prognosis

You accept the coffee, declining
the menu with minimal gesture, then
frown as I place gold coins on the table
I don't want … anything, you say

We don't notice the ten am rush as
we measure our words
with resolute precision, stalling
and starting, clinging to script.

You disappear into the street, drowning
in the traffic, leaving
me to walk the other way.
I wish you'd let me say goodbye.

Thereafter

Richenda Rudman

1.
Night. Moon.
Tight coils of misery find me in a suburb of red brick boxes,
creeping down a concrete driveway to the closed door of our place.

I yearn for boot prints on the step, or the door scratched with verse or heart,
but there is only a flower pot bought in joy, bought with plans
— a dried stick memory.
Under cover of dirt are the twisted butts of your cigarettes;
I dig them out, line them up under the moon's torch,
hoping to evoke the press of your lips.

And in a ripple cold shroud, I realise the madness of this,
and carry my shame away on tiptoes.

2.
Wet Monday. Sydney.
I'm on a bus, post-art gallery—sent there by my mother
for soul succour, for palliation.
The paintings have not spoken, nor healed
and I watch, with envy, as raindrops evaporate on the window.
A buttercup-yellow car stops on the street
and you emerge, wearing your blue shirt.
Later, I know I have been the screaming woman
begging for the bus doors to be open.

3.
Lunch. Family
I have no memory of asking my brother to take my dress for dry cleaning.
He follows up, helpful. The family looks at me, hopeful, as I scramble
the mish mash of cue cards in my head and find no dress, no dry cleaners.
And then they shrug, collectively.

4.
Anniversary. The Third.
Your face was not in the clouds, or the crowds.
I carry the relief of that.
I carry the relief and the sadness of that.

Not Forgotten, Never Known

Rebecca Douglas

Short of you running a crime syndicate from your living room, everyone knows what it means when the police come knocking. In March 2013, they told me my dad was dead.

I paused, unsure of the proper protocol, and settled for shocked stoicism. The police officers seemed both relieved and unnerved by this response. They beat a hasty retreat.

Dad had died in Longreach, a 6-hour flight. He'd spent his life travelling Australia searching for work shearing and fruit-picking before retiring to a run-down shack in his hometown that probably should have been condemned.

On the flight over, my mind flitted back to the last time we'd spoken, ten years prior. At uni, I'd dated a rich boy whose mum was trying to starve him into getting a part-time job. I'd bought him a spring roll for lunch. When I told Dad, he screamed obscenities at me and never spoke to me again.

In the intervening years, a nurse in rural Queensland called one night, saying my father had been in a car accident and his leg had been crushed, but he'd live. She asked if I wanted to speak with him. Instead, I left my number in case he wanted to call me. Silence.

And now, death. I arrived in Longreach and set about trying to honour Dad's wishes. He'd always been emphatic about having a no-frills funeral. He barely even wanted the essentials.

One day when I was a teenager, he'd specified his funeral preferences as I sat in his filthy Econovan. I was to dig a hole, kick him in, and shovel dirt on top. No preachers, ministers or shamans of any kind, not even a non-religious ceremony.

In reality, how would this work? I could hardly nick a neighbourhood wheelbarrow and trundle his rather substantial corpse from the morgue to a random patch of scrub for a bush burial. Apart from the logistics, there was a matter of propriety. When I met with the local council, they were keen to steer me back towards a more conventional method of mourning. I consulted a civil celebrant, who agreed to perform a short graveside speech. She ran me through a standard list of questions.

She was a beautiful, non-judgmental soul, but even she couldn't help but raise an eyebrow at my sparse knowledge of my own father. How did my parents meet? Don't know. Where were they married? Don't know.

What was his happiest memory? I really didn't know.

In the end, she did an admirable job cobbling together my pathetic personal snippets into a semblance of a eulogy. There's only so much you can do with 'He liked yellow and Janis Joplin and John Wayne', though, before the material stretches thin.

To my surprise, a handful of old fellas he'd gone to school with turned up. They seemed satisfied with the low-key tribute.

As for me, I wrapped up my trip and tried desperately to remember a man I had never known.

Slow time

Yvonne Patterson

after her memorial service, voices

entwine in whispers, flow
over tables, littered
with left-over food

tears of liquid cream bathe
crumpled scones

unfinished wine   sighs
lost in glasses

dust motes pirouette in twilight chords
trespass onto armchairs'
body dimpled seats

ephemeral dancers
in snow globes   suspended

time threads
through mists of liquid mercury

we tiptoe
through rooms mapped in memory

Grieve

Antonietta Franks

'I'm leaving and never coming back.'

It's sunny, hot. Kids are playing outside. Washing is dry, taken down and in the wash basket.

What will we have for dinner tonight?

I start folding clothes. Kids run in, run out. I'm tired. I hear him come home. Finds me in the laundry.

'I'm leaving and never coming back.'

'What?'

Front door slams shut. I hear his car drive off.

He's leaving? Is that what he just said? Is it because of the fight we had yesterday? But, we always fight.

Clothes now folded. I start dinner. Kids still playing.

'Come on in now. Wash your hands. Dinner's almost ready.'

5.30 pm. Dial his number.

'Dinner's ready. Where are you?'

'I told you. Not coming back.'

How do you grieve for unexpected and sudden loss? He's not dead. I can't bury him. I can't mourn. I can't put a notice in the paper. I can't have a mass. I can't read a eulogy and say all the nice things that are usually said about a loved one.

He's just gone.

House is empty.Kids are quiet.

What is he thinking? Where is he? What is he doing?

So many unanswered questions.

Heart is sore. Head is full, hurting. I'm tired.

I can't say goodbye. I can't look at photos. I can't listen to music. I can't watch T.V. I can't read. I can't talk.

What is grieving?

Please tell me so that I can start.

Sweet Pea

Josanne Ryan

The doctor's troubled face, his words, 'A matter of days, the kidneys have failed.' My mother's eyes, those wide orbs of blue, spoke of her knowing. She took my hand, 'It will be ok.' So like her to feel my heart tremor there in that emergency room. Decades of lithium had taken its toll. Now the cancer. Nothing would ever be right again.

After, the remembering kept me trapped. The questions pecked at me like buzzards, greedy for all I had failed to ask her. All her heart's stories from that long traverse of living. How the black dog had tormented her, how she'd struggled. There was a time when she lost her will to fight, my father finding her just in time. His heart shattered, he had waited for the coma to abate, not knowing then that she was to outlive him by another three decades.

It was the reverse of her wishes. The child in me can hear her chiding him, never, ever to die first. Not his choice, fate played that hand. The one who had sought to escape was to be the survivor of the pair. She lived a great innings, people would say. I barely know the half of her story; others far less.

Memories have stalked me, hurling me back beside her to that puke-green room. Heart-struck as she lay there, arms flailing, all deep moans and delirious rants. Those eerie nights, the hospital corridor's fierce light stabbing my streaming eyes as I wandered in search of help, desperate for the doctor's magic potion to ease her throes. My pleading to end her torment, wanting to set my mother free. Yet longing for her to stay, forever.

There was no sparing her. 'Come with me!' she'd pleaded in panic. All I could offer was 'I love you.' Pearls torn from the mangled shell of my heart. Her lightening quick reply, 'I love you more.' Then I was a child again, in her arms in the big bed, playing that game—our game.

Even now, years on, I fight the echoes of those long painful days and nights—the ending of her days. Instead, I yearn to be standing beside her, as I did as a child, amidst the riot of delicate sweet peas trailing skyward up the garden shed wall, watching as she cut me a posy. My teacher's bounty, those soft, jewel-coloured petals perched on long, slender stalks. Dainty beauties born of my father's toil.

It lingers with me still, her eye for beauty. How she laboured over lovely things, only to gift them away with the purest heart—a linen hanky edged with delicate hand crocheted lace or a nightdress embroidered with dainty grub roses. How I'd find a bunch of tender violets waiting beside my bed, a silent gift for returning home, a woman now, yet always a child grown of her. The missing, always.

Most of all I remember that she loved me. More.

Decay

Peter Erskine

Skin tissue-thin trips and tears
a Rorschach bruise all purple hues
the needle seeks the vein that slips
then yields its precious flow
with tales to tell of body's drift
to ladder's lowly rung;
I spy it with those dulling eyes
slow-dripping taps of salt-laced grief
now sprinkle sinking cheeks
stubble's short sharp prick
all peppery and sparse;
limp hair the white of dirty snow
facial lines a map poor-drawn
the etch of burden's trek
hesitant bite of tannin teeth
grey-plugged and chipped
to sieve the tainted breath;
ears that hear
but never words
the blur of echo's wayward ring
as feet escape the doubt of gait
a stick to beat the practised fall
before the arms of Earth embrace
another bag of bones.

Lipstick

Esther Ottaway

for Auntie Jenny

When Mum offered me your lipstick
I took it, like a fool, thinking it was just
a lipstick, thinking I might make use of it –
we were never a family to waste things.
I pulled off the cap to check the colour –
a gentle pink I could wear with anything –
and into my handbag it went. It's only now
in the morning rush in the chilly bathroom
as I press its shining cream along my lips
as its powdery scent releases and you come to me,
    standing on your tippy-toes
    to wrap your arms around my neck
    pressing your cheek soft with powder
    and wet with a visitor's tears against me
    my nose in the folds of your elegant scarf
    in the scent of clean linen as you say
    I love you so much, I'm sorry I can't be here more often
    and you kiss my cheek with this, this very lipstick,
it's now that, under my ribs, my disbelief that you have died
breaks, and I'm held in the mirror, soft-lipped, crying.

SGRS

Kane Stewart

I am an indentured servant,
I am supposed to be grateful that I'm no longer a savage,
I am a child, my sisters try to protect me from the mission boss,
His leering eyes, the smell of his breath on my neck burns hot,
I pretend to be asleep,
In the times of the night when he creeps,
I will never forget that smell, it reeks!
This month I missed the date,
It is now too late,

I am a station hand,
I work with all the cattle, sheep and their lambs,
I am paid in tea, sugar and flour,
My white counterparts get paid more for the hour,
Slaves my mob are, we were all black birded,
If I tried to leave, I will be shot as a deserter,
One of my friends tried to escape past that gate,
The police did find my dear old mate,
He is never coming back; it is now too late.

I am a new mother,
They take my child and give her to a stranger,
They say I am a bad parent and I will soon forget her,
They say I didn't care and gave her up in the letter,
But it was I who chased down the car as it sped up faster,
All I cried was 'No!', 'Stop!' and 'Wait!'
But they wouldn't slow down, she is gone and it is now too late.

It is now the present, the future,
The New South Wales government makes me an offer,
The Stolen Generations Reparations Scheme,
I will receive compensation for all those harsh and terrible years,
However, I had to have been removed before 1969,
Victory and justice are just never mine,
Despite the K. Rudd apology, acknowledging all the history,
I was removed in 1970,
One year off the date,
It is now too late.

Graveside Reflections

(A Haiku Trilogy)
Kathryn R Bennett

1.
Mandala
Petals in patterns
Blanketing your earthen bed;
Short-lived beauty shared.

2.
Dragonfly
On gossamer wings
Our parted spirits commune
Across Death's membrane.

3.
Passing
Mourning, once sharply
Engraved on headstone and heart,
Mellows and weathers.

La Vie En Rose

Kate O'Neil

Jennifer (Oct 1954 – Dec 2019)

In this time of several griefs
am I asking too much of my roses?
I would like them never to fall,
to stay, strong and vigorous,
snagged forever on the hem of November,
with me.

I plead with them,
heap on them care and praise,
feed them, clear every weed.
tell them I need them.

–

All through those first December days
when we three watched
the darkening smoke of bushfires,
the roses flourished:
Happy Child, Earth Angel,
Blue Moon, Heritage, Heaven Scent.
La vie en rose…

The third day was your last.
You said 'Goodnight' and
a moment later you'd gone,
your slumped body
quite empty of you,
and you oblivious to
either roses or fires.

For weeks green eucalypt forests
burned to blackened poles,
ash fell, while we longed for rain,
and you,
and through the heatwave,
my English roses bloomed,
denying this laying to waste.

In January we drove,
two of us,
through blackened firegrounds,
to the holiday house
for three.

Somewhere in the desolation
around the charred remains
of December's lost houses,
I knew there would be
ashes of roses.

The List

Joshua Wildie

When he woke up in bed alone, he didn't wonder whether she was in the bathroom, or already having breakfast. Instead he picked up the notepad and ticked 'Realise Ellen isn't coming back' and then he got up and ticked 'Wake up before seven'. His back and neck were stiff and sore, but he supposed better than yesterday. He didn't feel like doing his recommended stretches, but the physio would be on his case if he didn't. Plus, each stretch got a tick.

She used to make fun of his lists, but they got him through the messiness of a day. A way of focusing on one step at a time. The satisfaction of crossing something off created momentum for him to keep going and achieve more. So naturally, after weeks of being overwhelmed, he resorted to making lists again.

After eating some toast for breakfast (tick), coffee (tick), shaving (tick), combing hair (tick), flossing (tick), brushing teeth (tick), taking antidepressant (tick), painkillers (tick), he got into the shower. The lukewarm water rained down on him. When he finally picked up his shower gel, he realised the bottle was empty. Ellen's various skin and haircare products still bordered the shower floor. He'd been unable to tick 'Move Ellen's belongings' for a few days now. He picked up a coconut and lime body wash and squirted some in his hand. The scent brought her face to mind in vivid detail. The feeling of running his fingers through her thick brunette hair. That smell filling his nostrils as he kissed her neck.

Without applying any to himself, he threw the glob of body wash on the wet tiles and the shower ended suddenly. He redressed in the jeans and shirt he fell asleep in. The images of her body were still there when he took two cups out of the cupboard. He placed one back, turned on the kettle and took a deep breath. He took out the list and wrote 'Buy shower gel' and underlined it. When he looked up, he saw out the front window into the empty driveway. Thought of his old Civic being parked there. The two of them heading to the shops. Him driving. The difficulty of backing out when everyone parked up and down the street. Fiddling with his iPod. Not seeing the Hilux until it slammed into the passenger side.

The list had been scrunched up and thrown across the room before he could stop himself. He took more deep breathes and picked up the ball of paper from under the coffee table. He flattened it and scoffed at the goal, 'Drive'. Chances were her Corolla would remain in the garage.

It was best to keep the goals small and achievable. Realistic. Don't write 'Drive'. Write 'Go in garage'. Not 'Return to work'. Try 'Call someone'. Don't write 'Be happy'. Start with 'Get by'. Don't write 'Move on' until you can tick 'Mourn' and then 'Accept'. Perhaps, one day, 'Forgive yourself'.

Until

Fiona Lynch

(For Terry).

an ardent Perth sun bites deep into backyard concrete,
stubble lawn and chancrous burs mock bare feet,
fooled by the soft promise
of salt 'n pepper sand under the swing;
naked metal cries in the summer wind and toes bleed secretly

near-enough flattened nail heads
threaten to trip him on the cubby steps
watch he doesn't hurt himself
. . . from the kitchen where
curried cabbage swims
in a luteous sea of mince globules

below the ledge, a weedy blistered boy—
three
and already walking like a visitor in his body;
the director's cut of a brother, china blues
hypnotised by the workings of a hose,
his fingers caress the nylon cobra
and try to hold the capricious column,
repeated attempts with stealth
as if somehow trickery might catch it off guard—
playfulness, intrigue—
it appears solid
until
it falls through his fingers

twenty-four years on
the cynosure of our eyes are given over
to the bardos that he calls in
with a loop of a serpentine hose,
floes of ice cut through—
he appeared solid
until
he fell through our fingers

Flesh

Andy Jackson

for R.

it feels meaningful but isn't   the ornamental plums
dropped   crushed   at the feet of their trees

cockatoos want the stone not the flesh   there isn't
anywhere clear to stand   it's all a mess only the ants

and the earth will accept   how have you managed
to cross the churning cold strait   with that fresh hollow

torn into your body   already your mother's
jumper is losing her scent   a snippet of her hair

curled into a box   you could say we're both
at home now   but we own nothing   and death

has eaten holes into our clothes   the fly-wire   our skin
the backyard a carpet of bitter debris   and I want you

more than ever   and the world is all flesh

of love & physics

Anna Murchison

the night of the day you died, the moon came
up huge and full—a blaze of orange in a cloth-
hung sky—and I thought, as I have often done,
that no one lived is ever gone. you were there in
the moon as you are here upon my tired skin, and
in the dirt and the dinner and the driving
rain and in the hither-slick of engine oil I
narrowly avoided as I drove our warring
children home. such things as these confirm
(much as your betrayals did) what I know of
love and physics—which is,

they are one and the same.

grieving

Jan Napier

from above, the sky is not blue,
it is pacific and indian, and the little sea
of aral, which shrinks and shrinks until it is just
a brooch pinned to a russet cloak

and it is raining

it rains like a piano,
like a rhapsody, a carnival, a pearl,
it rains like velvet, like a map, like a story,
every word its own history

it is the rain that the deaf know

and the very young
who know how to listen to silences behind the said
and the spreading wetness, who fly the second sky
bared in puddles

this is a thousand year rain

a rain that will fall forever,
while the seas, the black, the caspian, even the salty dead,
which are not blue but purple and silver and teal,
all swell and swell

rain makes and unmakes the world

An Uncertain Place

Deborah Norrie-Jones

The world is an uncertain place,
moves in a linear fashion
but then round about trips back
on itself.

Like the thread in my old Singer,
(in the wrong place, at the wrong time)
tripping the bobbin and spinning out
knotted tension.

Sigh, pull it apart, cut out
the knot, the clot,
cast away tangled threads, too hard
to bring to reason (separate, smooth out,
return back to how it was).

Too hard to look heroin
straight in the eye of the needle,
that went back
again and again,
into the arms
of my son,
until all the live threads
in his body were blue.

On Looking into the Wind

Peter Ramm

And not to think of any misery in the sound of the wind —Wallace Stevens

The town is a cold sweat, casting off the dregs
Of summer, mercury sunken like the long night's dew.
The air is cool, and the sun slants in the Western sky,
Making of the trees a fallen squadron of Spitfires,

Nose down along the road. The pied cormorant
—Survivor of January's tribulation has become a ghost
At the dam's edge. Winter begins to suck the green
From the kangaroo grass and rye, and at the servo I see

A tourist eclipse himself inside his puff jacket. The breeze
Follows the curve of Kangaloon gully until it bursts
The highway's bitumen seam and slaps at the tourist's
Face: Persephone passing; Demeter's despair—the cool

Trail of air dancing off her heels on her descent
To Hades. How beautiful the crab apples' leafy skirts,
Fallen around their ankles. The country quivering
Turns me nakedly home, to you, to your sharp skin.

Once . . . Now

Elizabeth Macintosh

As a teacher who retired from full time employment, I have discovered the unexpected grief that accompanies the transition to casual work.

Once, I felt valued and appreciated by Year 12 students. After I retired, countless teenagers begged me to return and complained that my replacement wasn't teaching them properly. Now, three years later, most aren't interested in what I have to say and want my replacement instead.

Once, students arrived at my classroom door with a smile on their face and appeared pleased, at least outwardly, to see me. Now, some arrive, their faces drop, they pull a face and say, 'Oh, no.' Some even walk away and attempt to truant. That hurts. My self-esteem is shattered.

Once, in 38 years of teaching, I could only remember one student who swore at me. It was so uncommon that I could tell you his name, where he was sitting and that it was last period on a baking hot Friday afternoon. Now, I am lucky to survive one school day without being sworn at, usually by a Year 9 boy and often involving the 'f' word.

Once, students rarely complained about the content of my lesson or the work they were required to complete. Now, it's unusual if they don't complain, even if the lessons have been provided by the absent teacher and sometimes simply involve watching a documentary or movie.

Once, I expected to be chosen to replace absent staff because of my wealth of experience. Now, others are called first, even those not trained in the relevant subjects. I'm not young or pretty or slim. I'm not good enough anymore. I'm nobody now.

Once, colleagues sought my opinion on myriad of topics because they valued my experience and knowledge. Now, they seldom ask. Perhaps younger teachers feel threatened or know it all or think that when I retired, everything I knew evaporated from my brain into the ether.

Once, students listened to me and wanted to know more about the topic under study. Now, most would rather keep talking and socialising. Occasionally, they even laugh at me, not with me. This is despite receiving a handwritten commendation personally addressed to me by former Prime Minister Gough Whitlam for 'producing exceptional students', surely a rarity in a rural secondary school.

I grieve the loss of relevance. I grieve the lack of appreciation. Most of all, I grieve the way teaching used to be.

Different

Sophia Moore

When all your prayers
are answered

Yeses and nos
(mostly nos)

And you speak of when
you were young

You will think of
her

Differently

But you will
still
think of her

One Request

Damen O'Brien

if I am allowed

I would have that time you rested your head on my chest and I

stroked your hair

when everything else which was worthy

has gone into that dissolution which cannot mourn itself

I would have that moment survive

whatever could be worth our elaborate pains

if the universe forgets even this

I would not ask for anything else

what would be worth a billion years of falling stars

and the long night after

if nothing remembers

I stroked your hair

Puzzle

J V Birch

I'm the jigsaw I didn't buy before lockdown with plenty missing
and barely any sky but there's some crazy-ass clouds
being pummelled by the sun and something with
feathers so it's got to be grief and I try to do
the edges first like they say you should
but most pieces don't fit and others
won't stay and it all gets a little
too much when I find bits
of me for days weeks
months after and
realise how it
is that we
do this
alone

Goodbye

Dianne Montague

I was ten when they told me. *'Your Pa has passed away.'*

I remember you Pa as a gentle man. You gardened by the phases of the moon. Your smile and hugs softened the chaotic world. Dad had left when I was two but you were always there. Then you weren't. I missed you so much. Life became very uncertain. People left when I wasn't expecting it.

I wish I'd said goodbye to you.

I was sixteen when they told me. *'Your mum has passed away.'*

You were always busy Mum. Working to support us, your two children. You lived in a whirlwind with no time for chats and hugs. When you married again we grew even further apart. Then you got sick. For those three years you were in and out of Hospital. I didn't understand what was happening. I just knew that you weren't getting better. Your death left me bewildered—searching for the mother I never had.

I wish I'd said goodbye to you.

I was eighteen when Nan told me. *'Your dad has passed away.'*

I wish I'd known you Dad. Every week my sister and I held your nicotine-stained hands to walk to your house and sit for those two hours. You were very tall and quite scary. You never explained why you left us. Then I left you to travel overseas with my Nan, after Mum died. You wrote several times that you were sick but not how bad it was. When I returned you weren't there. My questions will never be answered.

I wish I'd said goodbye to you.

I was twenty-two when they told me. *'He's passed away.'*

When I first saw you on the ship coming back from England I was instantly in love. You were tall and handsome, just like in the romance novels. I never dreamed you'd love me. We were so young when we married and moved interstate. You were my 'everything'—my reason to be alive. When the police rang to say you were in intensive care from a car accident, I dissolved. The two-hour drive to the Hospital was agony. Would you be alive when I arrived? I was by your bed every day for a week. You didn't wake. At night in my motel room I sat dazed. I didn't think I could survive the pain and emptiness after your death.

I wish I'd said goodbye to you.

I was thirty-four and by your bedside when they said. '*Your nan has died.*'

You were my constant support. I'd run home after school knowing you'd have a cupper and cake ready. We didn't share intimacies or feelings; your stiff upper-lip got in the way. But you taught me how to be strong.

I'm so happy I said goodbye to you.

The Specialist said. '*You have Prostate cancer.*'

I look at my companion, my friend, my lover of twenty years. He is accepting of his fate.

But I'm not ready to say goodbye.

Rose Madder

Jane Frank

You once told me rose madder lake was your
favourite colour. I always thought of tranquil
pink water, a canoe being rowed with paint

brushes as oars. You liked – I know – its fugitive
transparency, and showed me the way Turner
used it in his skies, explaining its powers of

granulation. I kept a sample you gave me with
its range of different depths. There's a photo-
graph of you next to my bed – I'd say you're

40. I see your cheeks and lips stained rosy
despite the sharp morning light. The mouth of
the *Girl with a Pearl Earring* was painted madder

lake, but I've learned that since. Vermeer used
rose madder to deepen vermilion, to stop the
rich colour fading, to hold memory in place.

Dragonfly

David Terelinck

This gift of sifted light
at the billabong's fringe;
it spills through casuarinas,
ochers the paperbarks.
Pobblebonk song bounces
across the black glass & I wonder
at all things trapped
beneath the surface.
A dragonfly skims the water's skin,
its leadlight wings flashing
in the late afternoon rays.

So pale & fragile
I can't help but think of you
in your final,
translucent months.
The way your skin contracted
to turn you inside-out;
the shout of each rib
& vertebrae.
I watch the dragonfly hover
for a second, then it dips & darts
& zips in all directions.
Conversation does not traffic
in straight lines either;
how we circled, side-stepped
the distraction & renewal
of disease & death.

The dragonfly disappears
with the fading light;
slips away like a final breath.
I peer into the darkness
aching
for one last glimpse.

Empty Chair

Evin Musa

My father was the most frustrating man to ever walk the earth. It's not just me saying, every single person who had the ambiguous fortune to meet him would agree with me. This includes immediate family members, extended family members, close neighbours, not-so-close neighbours, friends, his colleagues, the grocer on the main street, the president of the RSL club, the tea ladies at the church, and last but not least, every single one of the five cats that kept him company after mum died.

I can claim—with no risk of exaggeration—that I spent most of my adult life avoiding confrontations with him or apologising to people for his behaviour. He was never aggressive or explicitly rude to anyone but he somehow always managed to offend people beyond the tolerable range. It was as if normal social rules didn't apply to him. As if he had some sort of exemption to act and speak in a way that only suited him at the expense of everyone else. Case in point, about two years before his death, my sister cooked his favourite dish—slow cooked for five hours—and travelled thirty kilometres to deliver it to his door. She made sure she arrived at a time when he was awake. After many vigorous knocks on the front door, she got worried and went around the side to knock on the living room window. He opened the window, took the dish and shut the window on her face. Apparently she was interrupting his favourite 'Doctor Who' episode.

I never wanted any recognition for putting up with him, especially since mum died. After all, he was just an old man damaged by the 'Great Depression' and—probably—missing his wife. At some point, I found great comfort in believing he had Asperger's syndrome. That made things a lot easier. I started researching the condition very seriously and the more I learned, the easier it became to justify his behaviour. But then, very slowly, that comfort evaporated too. He became more and more unbearable as he got older and older. The guilt of avoiding him started bringing up old resentments. He never thanked me for nursing mum. He never asked if I needed anything. He never helped me through university. If my sister didn't intervene, he wouldn't have paid for my wedding dress.

I never wished him dead but I always thought life would be easier without him. I thought I'd miss him a lot less than missing mum. I thought I'd never miss hearing his deep voice or seeing his round face or feeling his big hands that he used to put on my face. I thought I'd just move on with my husband and my kids and my job and my friends and every other little thing that filled my life after mum died. I thought I'd never miss him but I was wrong. His empty chair breaks my heart now. I wish he was here.

Growing Old

Sue Pincham

We are old now. When we look at photos of ourselves, we cannot believe the person we are looking at is us. It is an old person. Not me, surely. Not us. We are not old old, (we think), just in our late '60s. But, truthfully, we are no longer young. The photos tell us that. Some of us have kept a handle on our weight, our hair color, plumped up our faces with botox or filler things, had a bit of a nip and a tuck. But I haven't. I look at pictures of me on my 60th, and I look happy enough, just fatter and older than I thought. Knocked around by life, so to speak. A bit worse for wear.

Within a small group of friends we have had the various cancers: breast, prostate, lung, melanoma. One of us has died, one of us has been told she is terminal.

For the rest of us, we have arthritis and various conditions ending with '-algia', all sorts of annoying and seemingly intractable body aches and pains. These days our ankles or knees hurt, our hips or shoulders, or it might be our back or neck. Even though some of us walk or jog or do yoga or tai chi and meditate, the bits still hurt us, and we are surprised. This wasn't supposed to happen to us. This only happened to old people and we really can't be old.

It is better with our glasses on, looking at the world. We see more clearly. But I prefer them off, when looking at myself. I see less of the sun damage and the crepey skin. It's not about vanity. It's about loss. I am reminded that my youth has gone.

Recently I was listening to the radio and I heard a writer say, 'Growing old is a series of losses.'

I look at my mother who is, of course, much older than me. She was incredibly vital until she was eighty, then her body started to give out. Physically she is infirm and housebound, although mentally she is still agile and intelligent. She reads the Herald back to front every day, discusses the news with my sister and I, keeps in phone contact with her friends. But she feels those physical losses in every bone in her body, in all her muscles and sinews.

Recently she said, 'I feel like I am just sitting around waiting to die.'

While her life seems almost pointless, painful, and difficult to her now, death still seems the less attractive alternative.

For my friends and I, we are old now, but not as old as we still hope to be. For we too know that life is fragile, and the next loss could be the final one.

Mowing the lawn

Beth Clapton

It ended, of course, we knew it would
yet I found myself unready
for the tasks ahead - how sympathy cards
would bury the lists and the aide-memoires.

The post has dwindled to dull brown
bills and periodicals, still every day
I make another call to unsubscribe
from the weight of it all.

The days lengthen, each skill I learn
I lose a little more, I pay the bills,
know the lawn can no longer be ignored.
I drag your mower from the garden shed.

It glowers at me from the lawn.
I should have listened way back when, instead
I watched a robin, hummed, relished the scent
of fresh cut grass, and you.

I coax the mower into life - it roars,
and I regret my surge of pride. With care
I skirt round daisies, buttercups
and dandelions already gone to seed.

Some days you can feel it slipping

Peter Lach-Newinsky

i.m. B. 1947-2012

Making coffee this morning, a black jumping spider like
a smudged M in 12 pt Arial moseyed along the plastic lid
of the electric kettle. As small clouds of steam began
to exhale from the spout, it drew inquisitively closer.
Buffeted at the volcano edge, it suddenly threw itself off
the towering metal cliff and, cushioned by its invisible
abseil, landed safely on the benchtop and slipped away.

These days the day may leap from its deep womb of sleep
texting new writing ideas, phrases, connections. Then
as the sun speeds west the hours harden into well-worn
tracks, texts, tantrums. There's the old withdrawal
into reading, writing, all the silent pleasures of the mindful
realms, soul-speak, the words' magic crooks and crannies,
tempered by tending two ebullient grandsons or the summer
orchard wild with birds and fruit. Books lured me early
from some grey ache I never quite understood, fantasy
more real than the real I met, dense with meaning missed.

Yesterday, I learned my first love had died, sixty-five.
Cancer. Diagnosed five years ago in the same wind-torn
winter I was, just after collusion and a tsunami melted
a reactor in Japan. This weighs on me like an invisible cloud
heavy with isotopes. She married, divorced, as we lost
contact, separated by hemispheres and diverging hopes.

Now I am that young, undying ghost forever breathing
her skin under the fine tent of her hair on the university
lawns, skipping lectures, filled with the first intensities
of our merging mouths, with love and those cellular codes
of scrambled letters untexting our far futures deep within.

Driving our slowly dying dog Billy for a huffing-and-puffing
walk half up the bush track we once ran along, this morning
old Dotty paused on the asphalt to let me pass. Long struck
by stroke, rain, hail or shine she slowly pushes herself shaking
along the roads, a walking stick-insect with a stick. Dogged
to move, determine her own direction, pushing her strong
will against the sliding slope of time, frail heroine
in floral hippy silk, bent forward into the indifferent wind.

Tragic Ripples

Muddling

The main street hum
descends on modelled malls and parking bays,
patterned by brick pavers
placed by the steady drone of men-at-work.
Commerce cranks, traffic nudges and creeps
needle-threading congested corners.

Yet here, my phantom friend
your eyes swim softly round Murrundi's bend
where Albert Karloan and Pinky Mack
final keepers of Ngarrindjeri law and language
hunker in their huts and endure white progress
with stoic black despair.

You've become one with history
all-seeing, all-knowing.
A bull whip rings.
Cattle are flicked and urged
past Mrs Edwards gate to cross the river.

You're quietly aware of ant-sized construction.
Bridge doggers and mates
sweat, bolt and strain the steel.
Every night they down their tools
and trudge away to weary homes.
But you are youthful, eternal, watchful
noting the echoed flutter of pigeons
roosting on chosen rib-cage girders.
They reclaim their squats, year upon year.

This is an ancient land, silent shadow
  You are now a part of it:
    a thread in its fabric
    a light dancing on its waters
    a ripple drifting through its currents.

Wood Gathering

Kat Beaton

I marvel at the hydraulic splitter as its terrifying wedge sinks cleanly into the huge rounds of chain-sawed wood. It's my job to pass them up to Dave beside me, who operates the lethal machine with a small lever.

'Want some gloves?' I ask, noticing a few cuts from the freshly sawn timber appearing on his hands. Maybe it's the thin skin that my dad tells me is all part of being in your seventies—he's always getting little cuts and scrapes too.

'Nah, I'm OK,' Dave insists. He says the same thing when I ask later if he wants some safety glasses.

There's a buzz of about 6 chainsaws and a similar amount of utes, all with trailers which are filling up fast with the split wood. Children, grandchildren, cousins, uncles, friends, neighbours, in-laws are working the chainsaws, the two hydraulic splitters and the hand splitters, or stacking split wood in the trailers. I glance over at Matt—with Jim's work jumper on and the chainsaw helmet, he's a dead ringer for his dad today.

My mind wanders as I'm waiting to pass the next round of wood. We're all here because Jim died. We're on this firewood-gathering mission because he can't do it anymore. We're taking this all back for Jill, because she needs the wood for the winter and Jim's not here to get it anymore. We're all here because Jim's not. I look around at everyone and it strikes me how much he would've loved this. Like a pig in shit, he would have said. He'd be on a hydraulic splitter, working like a Trojan and cracking jokes. He loved getting wood and he loved these good people who were his family and friends.

Fat tears roll down my cheeks as I pass another round to Dave. He can't see them, because of my safety glasses. Some blood from a nick on his ungloved hands drips onto the round and I point at it. He laughs. There's literally blood, sweat and tears going into this firewood. I so want to have a laugh with Jim about Dave's blood on the wood. I would've told him about it tonight around the fire over a whisky.

He would understand my tears, being a big softy himself. That was one of the things I loved about him—how he cried openly. Like when I stood with him looking at Nicki's artwork. He and Jill were moving into town from the farm and they'd had a big clear out, but he told me he just couldn't get rid of this big canvas she'd painted, not that long before she'd died suddenly, aged 21. We'd had a quiet cry together.

Somehow Jim's here in the midst of all these buzzing chainsaws. We're here because of him, working hard, filling the trailers. We know a big pile of split wood made him happy, so we'll keep working hard to make the pile even bigger.

Containment Lines

Tug Dumbly

It's the grace of the man that gets me, as he speaks of his three children killed by a drunk. Though that's not quite the right word. And although he has strength, it isn't the stoicism of a bloke trying not to cave in on camera. He has more, this man, some astounding epicentre of acceptance. He speaks of something irretrievable, but with this air of calm beyond ruin, like an old couple standing before the smoking remnants of their home, saying they'll start again.

Houses and land regrow. But this man and his wife, before a fence shrined with flowers and teddies, have less than a blackened paddock.

How does he do it?

Please don't interview him, I think . . . But he is mesmerising, with none of the scripted suffering to which he is entitled. He actually smiles, as he gives a little sketch of each gone child, perfect eulogies in a couple of lines. It's the simplicity and beauty he says it with that catch your throat. But mostly it's love. All this brokenness below, but the love and pride this young Lebanese-Australian dad speaks of his kids with overrides it. It's like he's smiling at them on a school speech day, and contains them like a rainbow.

Actually, it's mind blowing.

How is he doing it, how speaking, how breathing? But there is no bitterness for the drunk man who has done this to him, whose car ploughed through his life. That man is not part of this. There is something more powerful on the father's mind, an ocean of loss to be shored by love.

Somewhere, the man who did this got up that day not knowing he was going to destroy lives. Somewhere the man drank and somewhere, three times over, decided to drive. And somewhere his decision met the decision of the father who told his children they could go for a walk, as long as they stayed together. He said he wanted them to enjoy some freedom. Just as long as you stay together, he said.

If death's a dartboard, then that driver pricked the bullseye, which scored himself, along with those children and their families, their parents, brothers, sisters, grandparents . . . and on. The circles radiate out, pebbles on a pond, to friends and neighbours, teachers, coaches, doctors, police, emergency people, funeral people . . . into the hundreds . . . and still the circles ride out, in concentric waves, to people ticking names off school rolls, and people making little clerical deletions from government screens, and out beyond to all the farther suburbs of people like me . . .

And we're now in the thousands, as the little sum of one driver, three times over, four children, multiplies into what won't be contained, and radiates out to a huge arena, to fit all those people who heard the news, and saw the man interviewed and who wonder, like me, how does he do it? I wish he could teach me what he knows.

Edith Rachael

Jo-Anne Giles

Agett Way, Northam, 1995.

She barrels out the door in a panic.

The baby. Where is he?

The neighbours across the road note the thin material of her dress, her Hush Puppies, her unmatched socks, and call her daughter, Pat, who lives nearby. 'It's your Mum,' they say. 'She's on the move.'

Edith looks up and down the street, searching. Some phantom of the mind pushes her forward. She stumbles on the footpath and rights herself. She is looking for Jeffrey. He is calling out for her from some unseen rupture in time. He is drowning. She races towards the main street but she is really looking for the creek. That's where he is. He's soaked and cold. His lungs are filling with water. She must find him. She must save him.

Dargai Street, Moora, 1980.

There he is, Keith, her son. Her lip curls in contempt. His hair is long and straggly. He has a cigarette that hangs from the corner of his mouth and the ash hangs over her tablecloth. A cask of wine stands between them and he pours a glass.

His pockets jingle with coins and he pulls out fistfuls of change and hands them to Pat's kids.

My grandchildren.

He doesn't have children, of course, who would want him? If his mother can't stand him, what woman, what good woman, will?

'Edith Rachael,' he calls her. As if he too has rejected their relationship.

Moora, 1945.

The creek at the back of the old house is a lure for the children in the

neighbourhood, many of whom can't swim but love to throw rocks in the water. The plop-splash of a good rock makes a satisfying sound and Keith, who is five, often visits the creek. He likes the way the sun hits the water in the late afternoon. He has an apple in his hand for later.

He stops at the edge. Between the water and the grass. There is something floating on the surface. Initially he thinks it is a doll, not real. But as he wades out to the middle of the creek, he can see it is a small child and even face down in the water he recognises the little knitted cardigan, the blue hat. His stomach lurches and dread grips his chest. He turns the tiny body over. It is Jeffrey.

It is his brother.

He runs to the house to tell his mother. Her face turns a shocked white. She pushes past him and runs to the creek edge where Keith has placed the lifeless body.

She cries out in a strangled moan: 'No. No, no, no.'

Keith is frightened. His mother is bent over Jeffrey and she is shaking but there are no tears. When she turns back to Keith her eyes are deep in fierce rage. They grip him and hold him still. And she says it. The words that will reverberate through time and destroy them both.

'What did you do?'

Ink

Dee

I noticed it today. I really take the time to look at it, reflect on its meaning and the reasons why I had it permanently marked on my wrist. It's the first time in awhile, if I'm honest with myself. I've been so busy that I have to admit that sometimes I don't (or rather, I pretend the circumstances are different) and I've learnt that both of these reasons are OK.

I go through the motions of an ordinary day: I wrap my two favourite armbands around my wrist without a sidelong glance and I get on with it—life, that is.

I have a dental appointment. Over the years, I've become quite familiar with the two front office staff. They feel like friends.

I look down at my wallet, searching for my credit card.

'You've got new ink.'

More a statement than a question.

Amazing that she noticed considering how many clients she sees on a daily basis. It catches me off-guard.

I nod, a little lost for words and continue to search in my wallet, pretending to look for that card.

I finally hold out my arm; presenting her with the gift that I think it is.

She looks closer and I can see the questions in her eyes; can she see the same in mine?

'My best friend's son. He died last year; his mum, dad and I have ink to celebrate his life.'

'Can I ask how he died?'

Pause. Keep the voice clear; face straight. No tears . . . this time. Spread his message—continue to say his name.

'Nathan took his own life.'

Uncomfortable faces as they both stand there and look at me . . . another pause.

They don't know what to say, of course they don't. Who really does? It's up to me.

'It's OK. Please don't be uncomfortable. That's why I had this done. To start conversations; to stop the stigma . . . It's OK honestly. We need more people asking questions. We need more people to talk.'

I hear their breathe escape; exhaling like the air in a balloon after a kid's party and the thought ever so briefly takes me back to days of innocence before life changed forever.

'He was loved, but he was finding things difficult. He thought he could get better alone. We choose to say his name and talk about him; remember the good times and the moments when he was happy. That's how we honour him.'

And there we were in the dental surgery talking mental health, finding support, how it's important to connect with others. How it's OK to not be OK.

Reminding me, oh so beautifully about the ink on my wrist.

I meet the eyes of my daughter who had slipped quietly behind me into the waiting room. She nods at me and for just a brief moment, I feel our thoughts are parallel.

I take in the sunset that evening—Nathan's favourite part of the day—and I gaze at the ink on my wrist.

Doors I have walked through

Geoffrey Moyle

The door to the factory he worked in
As a young man
Before marriage, and after
Is gone now
And the factory beyond it too

He is not in the factory, or office
Or the machinery, or paperwork
Not in the measured estimates, in longhand
And old increment, and unit

Some of the work perhaps remains
If I trace it on distant canopied roads
Trees joining hands over me
And salvage use for aging frames and carcasses
He is in the doors I have walked through

Let Your Daughter Go, Find Autumn

Amy Wallace

Autumn steals the long days from Spring,
The dawn sunrise turns pinker in the reflection of water
And the morning air is crisper.
Was it Autumn that stole your daughter too?

The season turns, the season flees.
In the way the oak tree clings to its leaves,
You take caution in letting go of the last
Like the carefulness in letting go of your daughter,
You tried your hardest, but you never caught her
And as the new season arrives, you unpack
Your heavy coats.
You learn to get used to missing the warm sunshine
And on the days where the Autumn leaves fall harder,
You crave to listen to the sound of your daughter's laughter
Mingle with the sound of rustling leaves.

As Autumn deepens, your loss deepens,
Your grief deepens and
The colder days creep in.
Old oak now as naked as the nursery
Without your daughter sleeping
And Autumn winds howl, weeping,
Crying for relief from Fall's feelings
The way your daughter cried for healing.
Was it Autumn that freed her too?

The season stirs, the season goes.
In the way the oak tree regrows
You open your heart just as the clouds open
To let through the warm sunshine.
You see her in the playfulness of the world's colours,
You see her eyes in the shape of your mother's
Do you feel her in the Autumn too?

When Grief Fades

Mim

He scattered her ashes last Wednesday, by himself, from the top of a mountain. Sent me a photo of the view, a bottle of champagne and a solitary glass. He texted later in despair. 'Nothing's changed,' he said, as if the tipping of ashes would somehow eradicate grief.

I wanted to explain to him what grief was like for me and what it feels like not to be grieving. And all I could think of was that grief is anguish and it consumed my entire body, my mind, every waking moment and every part of my life. I found it in the music of Sibelius and others like him who wring the last cries of sorrow and pain and tenderness and aching love from the highest notes of a violin. The music of grief penetrates to the core. You grieve for your lover and you grieve for yourself; all those losses. Your life isn't what you planned or hoped; there is no plan B; you are alone, totally alone, no matter what family you have, or friends. You put on a good face and they tell people how well you are coping. But you know it's a farce. If that is not enough, there is a helplessness that you feel when you can't get the lid off a jar or the water pump breaks down and you can't fix it no matter how hard you try and you find yourself saying out loud, 'If only he were here, I wouldn't have to fight this thing.' Sometimes all you can do is wallow in grief. And sometimes you have to speak severely to yourself and just get on with it.

Gradually, grief subsides but sadness lingers. And the sadness and loneliness makes you cry sometimes, and sometimes can be often at first, but it isn't all consuming as it once was and there are many more good days than bad and it is bearable. And even on the bad days, you know it will pass. Although sadness remains, it doesn't tear at your heart or render you helpless, abandoned and desolate, as grief did.

I want to tell my friend that when grief departs, it may surprise. He will feel stronger, lighter. One day, when grief fades, he will find himself again, changed—yes, but able to face the world with a joy and energy he thought was gone forever. I want him to know that he will be okay.

Sober Sixty

Libby Sommer

Samantha's single women friends were envious although she assured them Johnny wasn't perfect. Mood swings, challenging stuff like that.

Nobody messed with Johnny. Nobody knew better than he did, he was always watching YouTube and learning new facts and figures. Also, he rode a motorbike and practiced shooting at weekends. There were Facebook groups for bike riders and a rifle range nearby. Johnny was proud of being a rev-head and a good shot with his gun and not many people could disagree that he had unusual interests for a man his age.

'Sober since forty and counting,' he said about his sobriety. They didn't talk about his twenties and thirties.

There's a photograph of the two of them from Christmas day. Johnny had tried to lower himself to Samantha's height for the photo so they'd be on the same level. 'Stand up tall,' she'd said. 'Stand to your full height.' 'That's right,' he'd said. 'You like things big.'

'What does ATP in ATP Cup stand for?' was the type of thing Johnny would call out while she poured him a glass of water before setting out on a stroll around the block.

Samantha thought she knew the answer, but didn't want to risk being wrong. She'd learnt to tiptoe around his wildness and dreaded the fighting when she wasn't attentive enough to his needs. Dry drunk, AA called it. The unpredictable rages were doing her head in. She knew she needed the courage to walk away.

Now she's getting by a day at a time.

Her friends say she's one of the lucky ones. She's dodged a bullet.

The Death of Memories

Christina Bowkett

He was dead before he died.

I realised this when I saw him cleaning out his shed and filing old papers accordingly, tying up loose ends, readying the place to be laced with a neat bow upon his actual departure. He was already gone.

I was eighteen. I learned that when a dead man takes your hand and starts swaying to the sound of an orchestra you can't hear, it's disrespectful not to sway along. I'm not sure where we were, but it wasn't the kitchen anymore. He was humming some tune and I was shuffling awkwardly on my feet. High doses of morphine can make people do that, apparently. The 'dying man' etiquette requires you to just play along.

It's the same etiquette that applies when a dead man asks you to speak his eulogy—before morphine is involved. You say yes, thinking you won't actually have to because he'll be too dead to know that you chickened out the morning of. He'll make sure others hold you accountable though; you speak with such eloquence in front of crowds and you're his only granddaughter. You'll have to do it.

Before he truly dies, the dead man tells you the two premonitions that he says the angels whispered to him. The first is that you'll be a famous actress and the second is that a large-scale earthquake will occur along the coastline of East-Asia. The tremors will be so large that Australia will be impacted and many people will die.

You wonder if the aftershock of the earthquake he predicted was so grand that it rebounded on the borders of time and found its way back to you in the moment you saw his coffin there. Perhaps you were the actress in some twisted movie, and soon someone would say, 'Cut!' as you hastily murmur through the eulogy. Perhaps every thought after the death of the dead man was a part of the eulogy, because everything was said in honour. Perhaps grief was never a feeling waiting to be felt—perhaps it was a slow-growing ache in your chest when you realise that the dead man is still alive everywhere you look, even after dying.

Perhaps.

The Pancake Dance

Tamara Lowe

I look for you always.

In the curls of my hair and the shape of my hands.

In department stores staring at your favourite fuchsia nail-polish.

In lyrics of songs you sang before you kissed me goodnight.

In a turquoise shirt, once yours, that I have kept hanging in my cupboard for twenty-five years.

I close my eyes and bring your pancake dance to life. Four frying pans cooking on the hob all at once! One hand holding the skillet in the air, the other tipping in drops of melted butter. You gently tilt the frying pan ladling batter in quickly, swirling a creamy layer over the base before placing it back down on the heat. While it cooks, you begin another wafer-thin disc in a different pan, all the while watching for the right moment to flip pancakes in other pans into the air, to land on their underside and cook a few minutes. This routine continues many times over until the batter bowl is empty and the stack is piled high.

You mix sugar and cocoa together in a jar, 'It will melt into chocolate sauce in the oven like magic,' you whisper into my little ear. When I am old enough, I help spoon lines of chocolatey powder down the centre of each pancake. You show me how to fold one edge over to form chocolate-filled semi-circles, then roll them carefully into pancake cylinders. You arrange them in your special blue dish and pour over cream ready for the oven. Chocolate perfume wafts through the house as they bake. All through my childhood, you danced your pancake dance.

My beautiful mother, destined to live only half a life. I held you as you lay dying in the hospital bed. Your once vibrant face swollen and still. Each day bringing death ever closer; time determined to collide into space, sending shockwaves of grief rippling through my heart forever. My hand caressed your forehead the night you took your final, slow, gasping breaths, weeks before your fiftieth birthday. My motherless life thrust upon me at twenty-two.

Time moved forward and many years passed. The mummy in the centre of my life became me. My children know you only from stories and photographs. Their long-gone grandma way beyond reach. No snuggling into your gentle hugs. No grandmotherly spoiling or sleepovers at your house. No visits to their school on Grandparent's Day. And no helping hand when I need it most. Many times, I am still left winded without breath, engulfed by the primal pain of loss. You were the best kind of mother a person could be. All I can do is bring you to life in the stories and songs and foods I remember. And tell my children often how proud you would be.

Untied

Dave Smith

You don't know her, but she knows you.
I bring her to you every year.

The string wound around her little hand
trails a silver balloon.

One year ago, late at night, your eyes weigh heavy
turning the pages as letters tremble and blur.

The siren's wail, a silent invasion
Cruel tendrils grasping, searching
pulsing, spreading through soft grey matter.
Interlopers, star-shaped cells
distorting the signals, disrupting blessed peace.

Twelve months, your sentence, twelve months handed down.
You lie quiet, desperate
staring at the pale wall
the tally of days trickling past.

Sick potions drip into your vein
The blade, sharp and delicate
promising hope
where no hope can live.

In twilight, you lie, you stiffen, you scream—let me go
Let me die

Yes, okay dear—let's go.
I'm here with you. I die with you
every night.

Until you depart, just two months shy
of the day you'd hold her little hand for the first time.

And we're here again, and we watch
the silver balloon untied, released from her grasp—it sways
hesitates, the trailing string catches, then curls free into the blue.

You don't know her, but she knows you.

She celebrates Father's Day
not in the warmth of your lap
but in the warmth of the sun
that washes over
the rock that bears your name.

Thoughts at a Funeral

Michael Metzger

At a funeral, the dead come to life. Not always, but often. They may last for just a short while or live forever hunkered into our aching hearts.

Each one of us is not simply different, but unique, one of a kind. Even those sharing the same genetic DNA, who look similar, even identical twins, are unique individuals. That means our relationships with one another are particular. Our understandings, our attractions, our actions and interactions are all distinctive, exceptional—and irreplaceable. These rare and matchless moments are therefore precious —gems wherewith we stud the tapestry of our interwoven lives.

To hear the words of others recalling the moments that mattered, is to overhear the dialogue between the living and the dead, to transcend time and space in the creation of an instant of recognition.

Grief is a sword. It pierces us with love and longing for what once was and is now lost; but it is also a reminder of what more we might have done, of what more was possible, what more might have been. So, while I weep for the sins of omission, I also weep for the sheer joy of the love that still is. Tears are bitter sweet.

It's strange how we should meet in death. We spent most of our life together until, for reasons we now can never know, that helix of our friendship split and laddered its separate strands into other lives. And then you died and we, unarmed, were left perplexed, suspended by your absence. Yet here you are with all our yesterdays shuffled into the present; today, when the image of your face reveals its likeness in the faces of your kindred; when your picture holds your gaze, frozen in its frame on the coffin.

I weep when I think of the time we lost, when I see the tears of those who lost you. A eulogy tells us nothing, its omissions are all the moments that mattered to each of us. Tears are more eloquent than words.

And then a cavalcade of mirages, each instant but a reminder of a larger scale, kairós, the lived time, the significance of the relationship that has already shifted to the next hazy picture. We are transported and we are lost. Later, by the grave, as the coffin is lowered, a child's voice pipes, 'Bye-bye' and we descend with you, bearing the flowers that will soften the clods of falling earth.

Though we are buried by grief, by regret and remorse, we live yet to recreate the days and years that were precious, times that will reshape themselves in our conversations and memories, that will now insinuate themselves into the fibres of consciousness and accompany us through whatever days we are granted. Throughout those days, we will test what we thought we knew, what we learned, how we should live—how we might embrace that moment that must come to us all, as it came to you.

when you died
the air around me
held your breath

Susan Chamie

www.ingramcontent.com/pod-product-compliance
Lightning Source LLC
Chambersburg PA
CBHW020640130726
47903CB00003BA/926

9780648850403